the WILL KIT

Second Edition

John Ventura

Dearborn
Trade Publishing
A **Kaplan Professional** Company

Editorial Director: Donald J. Hull
Senior Managing Editor: Jack Kiburz
Interior Design: Lucy Jenkins
Cover Design: KTK Design Associates
Typesetting: the dotted i

02   03   04   05   06   10   9   8   7   6   5   4   3   2   1

Library of Congress Cataloging-in-Publication Data

Ventura, John.
    The will kit / John Ventura.— 2nd ed.
      p.   cm.
    Includes index.
    ISBN 0-7931-4605-4 (pbk.)
    1. Wills—United States—Popular works. 2. Estate planning—United States—
Popular works. I. Title.
KF755.Z9 V46 2001
346.7305'4—dc21

            2001002368

Dedication

To my children, Stephanie, Erica, and Colorado

Contents

Preface

Most Americans die without having done estate planning of any kind, even something as simple as writing a legally valid will. Their failure to plan what will happen to their money, their home, and the other assets they own is sadly ironic. After all, just think how hard most of us work throughout our lives so we can buy a home—no matter how modest—lead a comfortable life, and have something to pass on to our loved ones! Yet if we die without having done even the most basic estate planning, we have no guarantee that our hard-earned wealth will go to the people we want to benefit from it.

There are many explanations for why so many Americans do so little estate planning. Some simply never get around to it, because their lives are so busy, because estate planning doesn't sound like fun, or because they think that they will have plenty of time later to do their estate planning. Others mistakenly view estate planning as something that only rich people need to do. Then there are other people who don't want to write a will or do any other kind of estate planning, because they are uncomfortable confronting the reality of their future death.

I hope that *The Will Kit* helps readers appreciate the fact that estate planning is something that anyone who owns assets should do—not just wealthy people. Planning your estate helps ensure that your loved ones will be financially cared for after you die, and that they won't be saddled with the kinds of legal and financial problems that can develop when someone dies without having done the appropriate planning. If writing a will is all the estate planning a reader does after finishing this book, I'll consider *The Will Kit* to have been a success!

I also hope this book helps educate readers about the wide range of estate planning tools available to them. Most people limit their concept of estate planning to writing a will, but in fact estate planning is much more. For example, it also includes purchasing life insurance, setting up a trust, and writing a living will, among other things.

I have two other, perhaps more unusual, goals for *The Will Kit*. First, I want to make the subject of estate planning as entertaining as possible. Therefore, throughout the book, I've included anecdotes about the estate planning of some celebrities and other well-known people. These include people as diverse as Elvis Presley, Humphrey Bogart, John F. Kennedy, Jr., Marilyn Monroe, Jerry Garcia, and the fabulously wealthy Doris Duke. Appendix A includes copies of the actual wills of some of these people.

Second, I want to expand readers' definitions of what they can include in their wills. Most of us tend to think of wills as dry documents that spell out in legal terms what we want done with our property when we die. In fact, your will can be much more. It doesn't have to deal with only your money, home, stocks, mutual funds, and other assets. It can be a very personal vehicle for conveying final goodbyes to your loved ones or for conveying special messages to special people. For example, perhaps there is something that you have always wanted to say to someone but were never able to because you were too shy, too embarrassed, or too emotional. Or perhaps you want to make sure that the important people in your life know just how important they are to you and why. You can address all of this in your will. When you include such personal messages in your will, it is no longer just a dry legal document but instead a very personal statement of your feelings toward those you care about most.

An important note about this book: Although *The Will Kit* provides detailed information about how to write a will and even includes sample wills, it is not meant as a substitute for an attorney's help. This book is intended to provide you with enough basic information about the subject of estate planning to make you feel comfortable meeting with an attorney and making informed decisions about your estate.

It's always advisable to get the advice of an estate planning attorney regarding the best way to legally transfer your property to others. Writing a will may be all the estate planning you need to do, but an attorney can familiarize you with other kinds of estate planning you may want to consider. Also, an attorney can help you identify potential estate-related issues you might otherwise overlook. Those issues could create legal and financial problems for your spouse or other beneficiary after you die, unless you deal with them while you are still alive. And best of all, the help of an attorney probably won't cost a lot.

Even if you are certain that you can write your own will, I advise you to hire an attorney to write the final version based on your draft. That way, you can be sure that your will meets the legal standards of your state and that it will achieve your estate planning goals. I hope you learn from this book and enjoy it, too!

Acknowledgments

My deepest, deepest appreciation to Mary Reed, who cares about this book as much as I do. Also, special thanks to estate planning attorney Jerry Jones of Austin, to estate attorney Jerry Frank of Austin, and to Carlos Barrera, CPA, of Brownsville, for their valuable input.

1

An Introduction to Estate Planning

This chapter introduces you to estate planning. It explains what estate planning is, why it's important, and who should do it. The chapter also discusses a range of tools you may want to use in your estate planning; however, it focuses most of its attention on writing a will since a will is the cornerstone of estate planning. This chapter also teaches you about state property laws, since the law in your state affects what you can and can't give away through your estate planning.

What Is an Estate and What Is Estate Planning?

When you hear the word *estate*, you may envision something big and grandiose and far beyond your own financial reality—a mansion, for example. However, in the eyes of the law, your estate is simply everything you own, by yourself or with others. Your home, car, furniture, bank accounts, jewelry, life insurance policy, retirement plan, stocks and bonds, and other assets are all part of your estate. Although some people have large estates worth millions, the estates of most Americans are relatively modest.

When we are young, we think that most of our life lies ahead of us and that we have a lot of time to worry about the somber details of deciding who will inherit our assets when we die. Therefore, when John F. Kennedy, Jr., and his wife, Carolyn Bessette-Kennedy, took off in their private plane in July of 1999 to attend the wedding of a relative on Martha's Vineyard, they had no idea that their golden future would end in a plane crash. However, Kennedy was different from many men his age—he *had* written a will, which is included in Appendix A.

Like most spouses, Kennedy left the bulk of his estate to his wife, Carolyn, and then to any children they might have in the coming years. His will also provided that if he and Carolyn had no children when they died, their assets would go to the children of his sister, Caroline Kennedy Schlossberg. In his will, Kennedy specifically left a scrimshaw set previously owned by his father to his nephew, John B. K. Schlossberg. As young and vital as Kennedy was, his will shows that he was a thoughtful and considerate man who understood the importance of setting out his wishes in a will. The tragedy of his death should remind us that estate planning, even just the simple act of writing a will, is an act of loving kindness for those we leave behind.

Like young Kennedy, if you care what will happen to the people you care about after you die, you must plan your estate while you are alive. The specific estate planning you do depends on the type and the value of the assets in your estate. Subsequent chapters of this book give you an overview of your basic estate planning options aside from writing a will.

Good estate planning lets you accomplish five key goals:

1. *Ensure that when you die, your property will legally transfer to your spouse, your children, or whomever you wish.* The people who receive your property are called your *beneficiaries. You* get to play Santa Claus!
2. *Provide for the orderly processing of creditor claims against your estate.* The probate process sets a deadline by which claims must be filed for possible payment. Creditors who do not meet that deadline do not get their claims paid.

3. *Minimize any taxes your estate may owe after you die, leaving more for your beneficiaries.* Tax minimization is typically a concern only for people with substantial estates. The section of this chapter entitled "What Is a Substantial Estate?" tells you more about larger-than-ordinary estates.

4. *Plan for the possibility that you may become seriously injured or ill and unable to manage your own finances.* Estate planning allows you to legally designate the person you want to manage your finances for you when you can't.

5. *Establish legal mechanisms to manage your personal and business finances when you are too ill or injured to do it yourself and to direct your health care when you are near death with no hope of recovery and unable to make your own decisions.* Without the appropriate legal mechanisms, your estate could be depleted by the cost of life-sustaining medical care and treatment you might not want if you could speak for yourself. You can use other legal mechanisms to help ensure the continued integrity of your personal and business affairs and to spare your family the difficult and emotionally painful decisions regarding your end-of-life care.

Planning your estate also helps bring you peace of mind. You can feel good about the fact that you have planned for the future financial well-being of your loved ones and planned for your own death, and that you have done what you can to ensure that your family won't face the legal and financial problems that could result if you didn't do such planning. In many ways, estate planning can be considered the ultimate act of love.

To help you further appreciate the importance of estate planning, Figure 1.1 provides a list of specific things estate planning can accomplish. Each of them is addressed in subsequent chapters.

Estate Planning Tools

A legally valid will is the cornerstone of most estate plans; however, it is only one of many estate planning tools you can use. Other tools include but are not limited to:

- Joint ownership
- Life insurance
- Retirement plans

☑ **FIGURE 1.1**
What Estate Planning Can Accomplish

❏ Provide financially for your spouse, dependent children, and others after you die. Financial planning is something you do to build your wealth. Estate planning is something you do to help ensure that the assets you accumulate during your lifetime go to the people you want to benefit from them.

❏ Arrange for the care and financial well-being of your young children should both you and your spouse die while they are still minors. Depending on your state, a minor is a child who is either under 18 or 21 years of age.

❏ Legally transfer your property to your beneficiaries.

❏ Control, even after your death, the access of your beneficiaries to the money and other assets you leave them.

❏ Ensure that the maximum amount of your estate goes to your beneficiaries rather than toward paying probate costs, legal and executor fees, and other expenses.

❏ Minimize the taxes your estate may be liable to pay and arrange for the payment of any taxes that may be due. Estate taxes are a concern only for those of you who have substantial estates.

❏ Minimize any delays in the distribution of the assets in your estate to your beneficiaries.

❏ Minimize potential creditor claims to your estate when you die and fund the debts your estate must pay.

❏ Plan for the future of your business should you become physically or mentally incapacitated, or in the event of your death.

❏ Arrange for the management of your finances and medical care should you become so seriously injured or ill that you cannot manage your own affairs.

❏ Plan and fund your funeral and burial or your cremation.

- Gifts you make while alive—*inter vivos* gifts
- Payable-on-death accounts
- Testamentary trusts
- Living trusts
- Living wills
- Powers of attorney, including a durable health care power of attorney
- Burial instructions

The right tools for you depend on, among other things, your estate planning goals, the size of your estate and the complexity of its assets, your marital status and age, whether you have minor children, and the needs of your beneficiaries. Over the years, as your wealth increases and as you acquire or sell assets, as your family grows, and as your circumstances as well as your family's change, your estate planning needs will change too, and it may become appropriate for you to use other tools in addition to a will in your estate planning. In fact, it is a good idea to periodically review your estate plan to ensure that it continues to meet your needs and reflect your wishes.

Looking at Kennedy's will, you notice that his estate planning involved more than writing a will. In 1983, when he was 23, he set up a trust. Among other things, the trust provided for any children he might have and for the payment of any federal or state estate-related taxes that might be due at his death.

What Is a Will and Why Is It Important?

A will is your legal voice after death. It provides you the opportunity to spell out what you want done with certain types of property after you die and to name the *executor* of your estate. This person will be in charge of your estate after you die and will be responsible for carrying out a number of specific duties. You can read more about executors in Chapter 3.

Other Characteristics of a Will

No will is exactly the same because no one owns exactly the same assets, has the same beneficiaries, and shares the same estate planning goals. However, most wills include similar kinds of provisions, including:

- A clause that the will is yours
- A clause invalidating all previous wills you may have written
- The names of your estate executor and substitute executor
- The names of your beneficiaries and substitute beneficiaries or the classes of your beneficiaries (for example, "all of my children")
- Exactly what property you are leaving to each of your beneficiaries
- Directions for how any expenses related to your estate, including debts and taxes, should be paid

- A clause that leaves to a residuary beneficiary anything that may be left in your estate after all of your other assets have been distributed to specific beneficiaries and after all of your estate taxes, fees, and other expenses have been paid

> John Kennedy, Jr., used his will to indicate to whom he wanted his estate to go after he died and to show that he had a special affection for his young nephew, the son of his only sister. His will also shows how much he trusted his cousin Anthony Stanislaus Radziwill, for he made him his estate's executor. He named another cousin, Timothy P. Shriver, as his substitute executor. The Kennedys are a very close-knit family and that closeness is reflected in Kennedy's will.

Writing a will is not just something that rich people or older people should do. Anyone who owns assets should prepare one. Depending on your situation, a will may be the only estate planning tool you need to use; however, if you use other tools—you set up a living trust, for example—you still need an up-to-date and legally valid will.

Being the parent of a minor child—a child younger than 18 or 21 depending on your state—provides you with a special reason for writing a will. A will provides you with a legal vehicle for designating the adult you would like to raise that child if you and your spouse both die. That adult is called a *personal guardian.*

If You Have a Minor Child and Do Not Write a Will

In many states, a will is the only legal vehicle you can use to name a personal guardian for your minor child. Therefore, if you and your spouse both die without having named a personal guardian for your child, the court will decide who will assume that responsibility unless a relative or close friend offers to take on that job and the court officially names that adult as your child's guardian. Bottom line: The person who ends up raising your child may be someone you do not like, respect, or even know.

If an adult relative cares for your young child without the legal designation of "personal guardian," problems could develop because the adult would not have a legal right to make decisions for your child. For example, she might be unable to add your child to her medical plan, register your child for school, or give her consent for your child to receive certain kinds of medical care. To get those and other legal rights, your child's unofficial guardian would have to initiate a court process to be named legal guardian.

Every state limits the total value of the assets a minor can own without having an adult to manage them on the child's behalf. If you write a will, you can designate the adult, or property guardian, who will have that responsibility. However, if you die without having written a will and the value of the assets your child inherits exceeds your state's maximum, the court will appoint a property guardian. This person will manage your child's inheritance until your child becomes a legal adult.

The adult the court appoints may be your spouse, a relative, a close friend, or a professional property guardian. That person may be the same individual appointed by the court to serve as your young child's personal guardian. If a professional is appointed, your child's estate will pay him an annual fee for each year that he acts as property guardian. If a relative or friend is appointed, she may or may not be a good money manager or she may not be someone you would want to entrust with that job.

HOT TIP

If your minor child is the beneficiary of your life insurance policy or annuity, the death benefits your child is entitled to won't be released until a property guardian or another adult with legal authority has been appointed to manage those funds on your child's behalf.

What Happens When You Die without a Will?

Understanding what can happen if you die without a will, or *intestate*, helps underscore why you need one. After you die, nothing may happen at first. No official will knock at the door of your spouse or send him a letter about the problems and expenses your family may face because you died without a will. However, your family may begin fighting with one another about who should get the assets you own, especially if your estate is substantial or if bad blood already exists within your family. Although that sort of conflict is possible even with a will, having one helps minimize the potential for conflict after you die. Also, trouble could develop eventually if your spouse or someone else close to you, like your unmarried partner, wants to sell or borrow against one of your assets after you die. For example, your wife decides that she needs to sell the home you both lived in so she can move into a smaller and less expensive place and can use some of the sale proceeds to help pay her living expenses. If you did not write a will giving your spouse full legal ownership of the home you used to share after you die, she'll have to take steps to become its full legal owner before she can sell the house. The delay may pose a financial hardship for her.

Another consequence of not writing a will is that your estate will probably incur fees and expenses it wouldn't otherwise. Those fees and expenses will be paid by your estate, leaving less of it for your spouse and other family members.

> Rock star Kurt Cobain took his own life in 1994. It was sad to see this talented new musician mourned by his legions of fans. After his death, it was determined that he did not have a will to provide for his wife, Courtney Love-Cobain, or their daughter, Frances B. Cobain. The petition for Letter of Administration revealed that this young man's success had generated an estate that exceeded $1.2 million.

And there are other consequences of not writing a will. First, a probate judge will appoint an administrator to perform the duties your executor would have performed had you named one in your will. That person may or may not be someone your family knows or trusts. Also, the administrator will be entitled to receive a fee from your estate for his services, which means that there will be less of your estate to distribute to your family members.

Second, the probate judge, not you, will decide who inherits the assets in your estate based on the inheritance laws of your state. Those individuals are your legal heirs. However, they may not be the people you would want to end up with your assets. Typically, your spouse and children are first in line to inherit your assets, followed by other relatives like your parents, siblings, nieces and nephews, and so on. The exact distribution pattern depends on the laws of your state. If you have no surviving relatives, your property goes to your state.

Other possible consequences of having a court determine who gets what include:

- Your surviving spouse may not receive everything you had intended that she would have when you died. For example, depending on your state law, your property could get split between your spouse and your children, possibly leaving your spouse without enough money to meet her financial obligations.
- Each of your children would probably receive the same share of your estate even though their respective financial circumstances might be very different.
- If you are in a same-sex relationship, your partner will receive nothing from the court. Unmarried partners, whether they are in a same-sex or heterosexual relationship, are not recognized by state inheritance laws.
- Relatives you don't like or maybe don't even know could inherit from your estate.
- The court will give nothing to your special friends, favorite charity, your pets, and so on. The judge is legally bound to distribute your assets to your legal heirs according to the terms of the law.

Get Legal Help

Theoretically, if your estate is relatively modest, your family situation is not complex—you don't have children from multiple marriages, everyone in your family gets along with one another, for example—and your estate planning goals are simple and straightforward, you can prepare your own simple will. A simple will is one that does not include a testamentary trust. However, it's best to hire an attorney to write a will for you. Although Figure 1.2 outlines numerous reasons why an

FIGURE 1.2
**Nine Good Reasons for Hiring an Attorney
to Help You Write Your Will**

1. It's easy to put off writing your own will. Hiring an attorney means you'll actually have a will.

2. An attorney will not charge you a fortune to draft a simple will, which is the type of will most people need.

3. With an attorney's assistance, you don't run the risk of preparing a will that won't stand up in court or that won't accomplish your estate planning objectives.

4. An attorney can identify potential problems related to your estate, as well as the solutions to those problems.

5. An attorney can tell you if you should combine a will with other estate planning tools.

6. If you are a business owner, an attorney can tell you about the special estate planning issues you face and how to address them. Those issues include business succession and liquidity.

7. An attorney can point out potential problems you might not think about if you do your own estate planning. For example, if you have children from a previous marriage and have remarried, an attorney can advise you how to ensure that they receive a share of your property when you or your current spouse dies. Without that advice, those children could end up with nothing if you leave all of your estate to your current spouse.

8. An attorney can explain how the probate process works and help you prepare for it. Probate is a legal process that affects the transfer of the property in your will to your designated beneficiaries, among other things.

9. If estate taxes are a concern for you, an attorney can help you minimize the amount of taxes your estate will be liable for.

attorney's help is advisable, perhaps the most important reason is that an attorney can help you ensure that your will meets the legal standards of your state and stands up in court after you die. If you write a will that is not legally valid in your state, it will not be recognized by your probate court and will be as though you did not write a will at all.

Procrastination is another excellent reason to hire a lawyer to handle your will, especially if you're a busy person. Let's be honest. If you're like most people, the last thing you want to do with your free time is write your will! Hiring a lawyer means that you'll actually end up with one.

A third important benefit of working with a lawyer is that she can provide you with estate planning advice and information you would never have access to if you wrote your own will. Among other things, for example, a lawyer should be able to help save your estate money on professional fees, taxes, and court costs. The lawyer can also point out other estate planning tools you should use in addition to a will; and if you are concerned that there may be costly contests to your will after you die, the lawyer can help you plan ahead for how to deal with them.

If all you want to do is write a will, if estate taxes are not a concern for you, and if neither your estate nor your family situation is complicated, you can hire a lawyer who is a general practitioner. Otherwise, work with a lawyer who specializes in estate planning law.

An attorney's help won't cost you a lot—probably between $100 and $1,000. Many estate attorneys will provide you with a will that includes a testamentary trust as well as a durable power of attorney and a living will for about $1,000. The exact amount you pay depends, among other things, on where you live—attorneys in large metropolitan areas tend to charge more than attorneys in more rural areas—the value of your estate, the types of assets you own, whether you are concerned that your will may be contested or that there may be creditor problems after you die, and whether the attorney is a general practitioner or specializes in estate planning.

Even if your estate is small, don't assume that you can do without an attorney. Bad idea! In fact, it can be argued that you need an attor-

HOT TIP

It is important to feel comfortable with the attorney you hire to help you with your estate planning because you'll have to share with him personal information about yourself and your family.

ney's help more than someone with a substantial estate. Consider this: If your estate is worth $90,000 and you make a mistake that costs your estate $10,000 after you die, your estate will be reduced by 11 percent. But if your estate is worth $900,000, that same $10,000 mistake would reduce your estate by just 1 percent!

To locate a qualified estate planning attorney in your area, get a reference from a friend, a family member, your CPA or financial advisor; contact your local or state bar; or go to the Web site of the American College of Trust and Estate Counsel (ACTEC) at <www.actec.org>. You can also write to the ACTEC at 3415 South Sepulveda Boulevard, Suite 330, Los Angeles, CA 90034.

What Is a Substantial Estate?

You don't need to worry about minimizing the amount of federal estate taxes your estate will have to pay after your death unless your estate is substantial. The definition of a "substantial estate" has changed over the years, but in the year 2001, when the second edition of this book was written, it is defined as an estate that is worth more than $675,000. Estates that are worth less than this amount do not have to pay federal estate taxes. However, in 2001 President Bush signed into law legislation that gradually reduces and then eliminates, for one year only, the federal estate tax. The law authorizes incremental increases in the estate tax threshold over time. In 2002 and 2003, the threshold is $1 million; in 2004 it goes up to $1.5 million; in 2006 it increases to $2 million; and in the year 2009, it goes to $3.5 million. The estate tax is eliminated in 2010 and then the following year reinstated either at a $1 million or $3.5 million threshold. However, depending on the political climate in the coming years, Congress could repeal or modify these changes. It is important, therefore, to stay in touch with your estate planning attorney.

For some of you, a car, furniture, and your household and personal items may represent your entire estate. Most likely, their total value does not come close to the threshold for federal estate tax liability. However, if you are a homeowner and if you have accumulated other assets like life insurance, retirement benefits, and stocks and bonds, you may be surprised to discover that unless you do the appropriate planning, when you die, your estate will have to pay federal estate taxes. Depending on your state, your estate may be liable for state estate taxes too.

If You Prepare Your Own Simple Will

If you decide to prepare your own simple will, before you begin take time to understand the laws of your state regarding what makes a will legally valid and the laws that apply to property ownership in your state. If you don't, you may end up with a will that is not legally valid or that does not accomplish your estate planning goals. The characteristics of a legally valid will vary from state to state. However, general characteristics are summarized in Figure 1.3.

FIGURE 1.3
Requirements for a Legally Valid Will

For your will to stand up in court, the following things must be true:

- When you prepare your will, you must be at least 18 years old and of sound mind. In some states, you must be 21 years old. "Sound mind" means that you are mentally competent—you are not senile, suffering from Alzheimer's disease or another organic brain disease, or mentally incompetent as a result of some other mental or physical problem.

- You must have *testamentary capacity.* When you write your will, you must know and understand the property you own and its nature; the people who would inherit your property if you had no will; and the plan you've outlined in your will to distribute your property to your beneficiaries.

- You must have prepared your will because you wanted to, not because you were forced to or because you were unduly influenced by others to write a will.

- Your will must include at least one substantive provision disposing of your property.

- You must include a statement in your will that the document is yours.

- Your will must include a statement that it is your intention to make your will your final statement regarding the disposition of your property.

- You must sign and date your will. In some states, your signature must appear in a very specific place, but other states don't care where you sign your will.

- In most states, your will must be written and witnessed. Most states require two witnesses but some mandate three. Typically, they must be at least 18 years old and must be disinterested parties, which means they cannot be beneficiaries of your will.

- You may have to have your will notarized, depending on your state.

You should also be aware of the federal laws that apply to estate planning. This book provides you with an overview of those laws. However, when you sit down to write your will, some of the laws may have changed. Therefore, before you write your will, get the up-to-date scoop on the federal laws you should be aware of as well as the specific details regarding the state laws you should be mindful of. Your state or county bar association may publish brochures providing this information. Another option is to schedule an information-gathering meeting with an estate planning attorney. Paying for an hour or two of an attorney's time before you write your will is usually money well spent.

When you write your will, use simple, precise language that leaves nothing to interpretation. Otherwise, your wishes may be misinterpreted and/or make your will vulnerable to contests from family members who were not remembered in your will or who are unhappy with what you did leave them.

Types of Wills

A typed will that is prepared in accordance with your state's laws for making a will legally valid is the best kind of will. You can write this will from scratch; you can prepare it using will-making software; or you can download a fill-in-the-blanks will from the Internet. You can also purchase a fill-in-the-blanks will at your local office supply store. A preprinted, fill-in-the-blanks will is also called a *statutory* will.

Fill-in-the-blanks wills are popular because they are so easy to use—you just fill in the blanks! Some dangers in using this kind of will exist, however. First, it may not allow you to meet your particular estate planning goals and address your estate planning issues. A "one form fits all" will simply cannot accommodate every eventuality and concern. Second, if you are not careful, you may use a fill-in-the-blanks will that does not comply with the laws of your state.

There are other types of wills as well, which may or may not be legally valid in your state. Also, some of them have serious limitations, so read this section of the chapter carefully.

Handwritten or *holographic* will. This kind of will is recognized by some states under certain conditions. If you handwrite your will, be sure to date and sign it. Make sure that the will has no other handwriting on it. If there is, the will could be declared legally invalid. However, many courts apply less stringent requirements to a handwritten will compared to a typed will when there is a question about the will's validity, assuming a court is confident that the handwriting is the will maker's. Among other reasons, this is because a handwritten will is such a personal document.

HOT TIP

If you handwrite your will and want to change something in it, start all over again. Crossing something out invalidates the will.

Oral or *nuncupative* will. Most states do not recognize oral wills. Those that do recognize their validity only in very specific circumstances, usually when a person is near death, has no written will, and has no time to write one. States that recognize oral wills often require that their provisions be put into writing soon after they are stated. Those states also tend to limit the total value of the assets and/or type of assets that can be conveyed by such a will.

Video will. If you create a video of yourself stating the provisions of your will, you have a video will. Presently, video wills are not legally valid in any state. However, a video will can be helpful if you're concerned that someone may challenge the validity of your written will by claiming that you were not of sound mind when you wrote it. A video of you reading your will might help prove otherwise. You might also want to videotape the execution of your written will as a defense against other possible challenges.

Married Couples

If you're married, both you and your spouse should have your own separate wills. It is not advisable to share a single or joint will even if you and your spouse own most of your property jointly. A key problem with a shared will is that your state may view it essentially as a contract between you and your spouse. If that is the case, the surviving spouse would be unable to modify or revoke the will as necessary.

HOT TIP

Although your will and your spouse's do not have to mirror one another, at the very least both of you should discuss your individual estate planning goals and concerns so there are no surprises in your wills and so you can coordinate your estate planning as necessary.

Wills and Divorce

If you are planning to divorce, consult with an attorney regarding how a divorce will affect your will. Depending on your state, a divorce may automatically revoke your entire will or just those parts of it that relate to your former spouse. Bottom line: You must write a new will or amend your existing will if you get divorced.

Information Your Attorney Will Need

If you hire an attorney to draft your will, you and your attorney will meet at least once so that the attorney can begin gathering the information she needs to write your will. In addition to finding out about your estate planning goals and concerns, the attorney will want to find out about your assets as well as your debts and your family situation. Figure 1.4 provides a more complete list of information your attorney will ask you to provide. Also, if you own a small or closely held business or have an interest in one, your attorney will also want the following, where applicable:

- Partnership agreement
- Articles of incorporation
- Shareholders' agreement
- Limited liability company operation agreement
- Corporate bylaws
- Business tax returns
- Buy-sell agreements

> **☑ FIGURE 1.4**
> **Information You Will Need to Write Your Will**
>
> ❏ Amounts and sources of all your income
>
> ❏ Amounts and sources of all your debts
>
> ❏ List of all the significant assets you own, their approximate value, and how you own them (joint or separate property, for example)
>
> ❏ The deeds and titles to or other ownership paperwork for all the assets you own yourself or have an interest in
>
> ❏ Current statements for any retirement, pension, IRA, or other employee benefits programs you participate in
>
> ❏ Life insurance policies—individual and group
>
> ❏ Current reports for any brokerage accounts that may be in your name alone or in your name and your spouse's (or another's)
>
> ❏ Current reports for all savings and money market accounts or certificates of deposit you and your spouse may own, in whole or in part
>
> ❏ Evidence of how all your checking accounts and bank accounts are held
>
> ❏ Copies of all trusts you and your spouse are grantors for or beneficiaries of
>
> ❏ Divorce decrees, property settlement agreements, and prenuptial and postnuptial agreements that you and/or your spouse may be parties to
>
> ❏ Any wills you may already have
>
> ❏ Any trusts you may have set up already
>
> ❏ Names, addresses, and birth dates of your spouse, children, and other beneficiaries
>
> ❏ Name and address of the person you designate as your executor

Legal Restrictions

No matter what state you live in, there are limits on what you can do with your will. For example, you cannot use your will to give away property that you don't own, nor can you use it to pressure one of your beneficiaries to take a particular action or behave in a certain manner that your state does not consider to be in the interest of good public policy. For example, it's likely that your state would view a stipulation in your will that your son can only inherit a certain sum of money if he divorces his wife as being not in the interest of good public policy because the state would not want to promote divorce.

In most states, you cannot use your will to disinherit your spouse. Also, you cannot use your will to leave an asset to a beneficiary for an illegal purpose or require that your executor use a particular attorney during the probate process. Some states also restrict charitable gift giving through a will.

What You Can and Can't Give Away with a Will

Depending on the kinds of assets you own and how you own them, you may not be able to convey all of your property to your beneficiaries using a will. Assets that can be transferred to others through a will are said to "pass under" the will or to be "controlled by" the will. They include assets that you own by yourself as well as assets that you and someone else co-own as *tenants in common.* (Ownership as tenants in common is discussed later in this chapter in the section on property law.) These are the assets that will go through probate when you die. Collectively, they are referred to as your *probate estate.*

Assets that cannot be conveyed to others using your will are described as "passing over" or "outside" the will. When you die, these assets do not go through probate but, instead, automatically transfer to your beneficiaries via some other legal process. If you include these assets in your will, the wishes you express regarding who should receive them will be ignored. Examples of such assets include:

- Property you own with someone else as *joint tenants with right of survivorship* or property that you and your spouse own together as *tenants by the entirety* (discussed later in this chapter).
- Life insurance proceeds
  The person named in your insurance policy as your beneficiary automatically receives the policy proceeds when you die.

> ## H O T   T I P
>
> You can name your estate as the beneficiary of your life insurance policy. If you do, however, the policy proceeds will pass *under* rather than *over* your will. Therefore, they will go through probate and will be subject to the claims of your creditors.

- Proceeds from any retirement plans, pensions, and IRAs you own that are payable to a beneficiary
- Informal trust accounts

    These are also referred to as payable-on-death accounts or Totten trusts. When you set these up, you must designate an account beneficiary.
- *Inter vivos* gifts

    These are gifts that you make to others while you are still alive. Once you have made such a gift, it is no longer yours to give to someone else through your will.
- Assets that you have placed in a living trust

    When you set up a trust, you designate a trust beneficiary in the trust documents.
- Partnerships

    Your ability to transfer your interest in a business partnership to a beneficiary through your will may be limited by your partnership agreement. Other property controlled by a contract may present similar limitations.
- Personal property

    In most cases, you can simply give away small items you own without leaving them in your will; these may include sentimental items that have little market value as well as other items of relatively low value.
- Your spouse's share of the community property you own together

    This is applicable only to those of you who own assets in a community property state. Arizona, California, Idaho, Louisiana, Nevada, New Mexico, Texas, Washington, and Wisconsin are all community property states. The rest of the states are separate property states. The difference is explained in a later section of this chapter.

> ### H O T   T I P
>
> If you live in a community property state and your will leaves your share of a community property asset to your spouse, that asset, depending on the law of your state, may not have to go through probate.

Wills and Single People

If you're young and single, you probably don't own many significant assets; therefore, writing a simple will is probably all the estate planning you need to do. However, as you grow older and your wealth increases, other estate planning tools may become appropriate for you to use.

> Marilyn Monroe, a 1950s sex goddess and movie icon, once said, "I don't understand why people aren't a little more generous with each other." Monroe revealed her own generosity in her personal estate planning, as you can see from reading the will she left behind when she died as a single woman the night of August 4, 1962 (see Appendix A). In that will, Monroe made special bequests to friends, but she also created a trust that would take care of her mother, Gladys Baker. Once her mother died, Monroe arranged for 25 percent of the remainder of her estate to go to Dr. Marianne Kris, Monroe's psychotherapist, to further the work of psychiatric institutions and organizations.
>
> Monroe once said that "Hollywood is a place where they'll pay you a thousand dollars for a kiss and fifty cents for your soul." Looking at her will and recognizing her caring nature regarding her friends and relatives, it seems obvious that Monroe may have sold a lot of kisses, but she never sold her soul.

If you live with someone in a committed, unmarried relationship, regardless of whether it is a heterosexual or a same-sex partnership, and you want to be sure that when you die your partner will be legally entitled to all, or a significant share, of your estate, you must include that person in your will. You may also want to name your partner as the beneficiary of your life insurance policy, pension, stock option plan, brokerage account, and so on. Additional estate planning tools may also be appropriate depending on your circumstances.

HOT TIP

Inheritance laws do not recognize same-sex relationships. Therefore, estate planning is absolutely essential for same-sex couples who want to be sure that their partners will inherit their assets when they die and especially if they have acquired significant assets together.

HOT TIP

If you leave all of your property to your unmarried partner rather than to your legal heirs—relatives who would inherit your assets according to your state's law if you were to die without a will—your will should clearly indicate that you do not want your legal heirs to receive anything from your estate. Otherwise, they might contest your will, possibly believing that you simply forgot to include them in it, or they might contest your will out of anger at not being remembered. By using your will to explicitly disinherit them, you discourage such contests, and if one of your legal heirs does contest your will, the disgruntled relative is less likely to prevail in court.

Understanding Property Law

How you legally own an asset affects whether you can give it away as part of your estate planning. Therefore, the next few sections provide an overview of your legal ownership options—different ways you can own property.

Because how you own an asset affects what you can do with it, when you are getting ready to acquire a new asset, it is a good idea to consider the best way to own it, especially if you are married or are living in a committed but unmarried relationship. Your options include owning an asset 100 percent by yourself or owning it with one or more persons.

Check your deeds, titles, vehicle registration, and other ownership documents to determine how you own your current assets. If you are confused, talk with your attorney.

Owning an Asset by Yourself

When an asset is 100 percent yours, you can do whatever you want with it. You can borrow against it, sell it, or give it away.

Joint Ownership

If you and someone else share ownership of an asset, you own it jointly. There are four types of joint ownership: joint tenancy with right of survivorship, tenancy by the entirety, tenancy in common, and community property.

Joint tenancy with right of survivorship. With this type of ownership, when you die, your share of an asset automatically goes to the owner who survives you. Therefore, you cannot give away your share in your will or by using some other estate planning tool. Bank accounts are often owned this way. Joint tenancy can be a good way for married couples and unmarried partners to own property together.

Tenancy by the entirety. Similar to joint tenancy with right of survivorship, this form of ownership is available only to spouses. When one spouse dies, the other spouse automatically owns the entire asset. Therefore, if you own an asset as a tenant by the entirety, you do not have to include it in your will and you cannot use your will or any other estate planning tool to give the asset to someone else—it belongs to your spouse. About half of all states recognize this form of ownership; some recognize it only as an ownership option for certain types of assets—real estate, for example.

Tenancy in common. If you own an asset as a *tenant in common,* your co-owners have no interest in your share. Therefore, you can leave your share to whomever you want. Owning an asset as tenants in common can be a good form of joint ownership for couples who want to purchase an asset together but are unsure about the long-term future of their relationship. John F. Kennedy, Jr., owned real estate with his sister, Caroline, as tenants in common. Even though he could leave his share of the real estate they owned jointly to someone else, when you read his will, you will notice that if none of the children he might have with his wife, Carolyn, survived him, he bequeathed the real estate to his sister.

Community property. With a few exceptions, if you are married and live in a community property state, you and your spouse each own one-half of the assets and money that each of you acquires together or separately during your marriage, regardless of whose name is on the ownership papers. Exceptions include assets you inherit and gifts you receive while you are married. Therefore, if you want your spouse to inherit your share of the community property, you have to transfer it to him in your will or through some other type of estate planning. The next section of this chapter provides additional information about community versus separate property.

Marital Property Laws

In the United States, there are two types of marital property law: community property and separate property. The type of marital property law recognized by your state affects what is yours to give away as well as the inheritance rights of your surviving spouse.

Community property states. As you learned in the previous section, if you live in a community property state, you and your spouse each own one-half of whatever income you earn and assets you acquire during your marriage. However, property you owned and income you earned prior to your marriage continues to be your separate property after you marry. Generally, if you move from a community property state to a separate property state, the property and income you acquired while you were living in the first state remain community property. There are exceptions to the rules, however. For example, if you receive a gift or an inheritance of any size while you are married, it is your separate property, not community property, and you can do whatever you want with it when you are planning your estate. However, if you deposit your inheritance in an account that you share with your spouse or if you comingle your separate property with your community property in some other way, the separate property can become community property. To avoid comingling, talk with an estate planning attorney.

H O T   T I P

You and your spouse can draw up a prenuptial or a postnuptial agreement to exempt certain property you acquire or certain income you earn during your marriage from the marital property laws of your state. Don't prepare such an agreement without the help of an attorney who has experience drafting such agreements. In fact, in many states, your agreement will not be legally valid unless both you and your future or current spouse are represented by separate attorneys.

In some community property states, community property does not have the right of survivorship. In other words, in these states, when you die, your surviving spouse does not automatically inherit your half of the community property you share. Instead, you must use estate planning to effect that legal transfer. Also, in these states, to help protect your spouse from disinheritance, you cannot give away your spouse's half of the community property unless he agrees to it. If you die without having conveyed your half of the community property to your spouse in your will or through some other legal mechanism, your state law probably entitles your spouse to receive your full share anyway unless you have children. If you do, then your spouse and your children could end up as co-owners of your community property. This arrangement could be problematic if your spouse and children do not get along. Therefore, be sure not to overlook community property when you do your estate planning.

Separate property states. If you are married and live in a separate property state, money you earn is yours only, and when you purchase an asset with your own money, you own it 100 percent; your spouse has no legal interest in it. If you both contribute money to buy an asset, legally you both own it, assuming each of your names is on the title, deed, or other ownership document. However, if your name only appears on the ownership papers, you are the legal owner, not both of you. For example, assume that you and your spouse pool your money for a down payment on a new car and both of you contribute to the monthly payments. Despite the fact that both of you pay for the car, if only your name appears on the title, you, not you and your spouse, legally own the car.

Community property can be changed into separate property. For example, you could give your community property to your spouse as a gift. To be certain that it is recognized as separate property, make the gift in writing.

HOT TIP

Consult with an attorney before changing an asset from community property to separate property or vice versa.

Where to Keep Your Will

Store your will in a secure and accessible location, and let your executor and at least one close family member or friend know that location. Your options include putting your will in a bank safe-deposit box, storing it at your attorney's office, or keeping it in a fireproof safe at your home.

If you are considering using a bank safe-deposit box to store your will, be aware that some states restrict access to a bank safe-deposit box after the owner of the box dies. Only after certain conditions have been met can the box be opened. This restriction could delay the start of your estate's probate process, which could be a burden for your surviving family members. One way to deal with this restriction is to make a copy of your will before you store it in your bank safe-deposit box and give it to your executor.

If you amend your will after you write it, be sure that you give a copy of the change to whomever has a copy of the will. The official term for a change to a will is a *codicil*. Also, if you revoke or cancel your will and write a new one, destroy all copies of your old will. If you don't, there could be confusion regarding which version of your will is valid when you die. That confusion could delay the probate process and the distribution of the assets in your estate to your beneficiaries. Unsigned copies of your will can also cause confusion.

HOT TIP

Don't make duplicate originals of your will.

2

Completing an Estate Planning Worksheet

Creating an inventory of your assets and your debts is an essential first step when you are preparing to write your will. Among other things, the inventory information is essential to assessing the value of your estate, determining whether estate taxes are an issue for you, and helping you evaluate whether you should use other estate planning tools besides a will. Also, creating an inventory helps minimize the possibility that you will overlook some of your assets when you are doing your estate planning.

This chapter includes an inventory worksheet you can use to organize your asset and debt information and to estimate the total value of your estate. Also, your executor can use your completed worksheet to help ensure that all of your assets are accounted for.

President Richard Milhous Nixon, the 37th president of the United States, lived 81 years. At the time of his death, he had earned an undeniable place in American history. Raised a Quaker, ambition pushed him forward through life. A few months before Nixon died, on April 22, 1994, he made his last

(continued)

27

will. He did not provide for his wife, Pat, because she had died the previous year.

As many presidents before him, Nixon faced the task of using estate planning to not only provide for his family but also to determine how the memorabilia, writings, and everything else he had accumulated throughout his full life would be disbursed. What is most interesting about Nixon's will is that almost all of the normal personal property that had historical or commemorative value goes to the Richard Nixon Library and Birthplace. The one exception is his "personal diaries," which are left to his daughters, Julie Nixon Eisenhower and Patricia Nixon Cox. If his daughters did not survive him, Nixon's will directs his executors to collect and destroy all of those diaries.

Another curious aspect of his will is that he leaves to his estate the proceeds from a lawsuit designated as *Richard Nixon vs. United States of America*. To this day the man intrigues us.

Few of us will ever own the kinds of assets that former President Nixon owned. Therefore, completing your asset inventory will probably be a relatively easy process for you. In fact, you may decide that you own so few assets that completing it is a waste of your time. That assumption can be a dangerous one. You may be surprised to discover just how much you own and the total value of your assets, especially if you are a homeowner.

Determining What You Own

It's time to begin the first step in the estate planning process—listing and categorizing your assets. Figure 2.1 provides examples of the kinds of personal property you may need to list on your asset inventory worksheet. Figure 2.2 is the actual worksheet. Ask your attorney for help if you have trouble completing the worksheet.

You will notice that the worksheet has spaces for listing and describing each of your assets, for indicating how you own each asset, for noting the percentage of each asset you own, and for recording each asset's estimated net value. Recording this information tells you several things:

> ☑ **FIGURE 2.1**
> **Examples of Personal Property to Include on Your Worksheet**
>
> ❏ Cash and cash equivalents, including checking and savings accounts, money market accounts, savings bonds, and certificates of deposit
>
> ❏ Furniture of significant or sentimental value, such as antiques, fine furniture, and family heirlooms
>
> ❏ Other household items, such as large and small appliances, televisions, VCRs, CD players and stereos, electric tools, sterling silver, fine china, linens, crystal, and so on
>
> ❏ Artwork of significant value
>
> ❏ Clothing of significant value, such as furs and vintage clothing
>
> ❏ Collections of substantial value, such as stamp, doll, and coin collections
>
> ❏ Fine jewelry or jewelry with sentimental value
>
> ❏ Vehicles, including cars, boats, motorcycles, and motor homes
>
> ❏ Stocks, bonds, and mutual funds
>
> ❏ Life insurance policies
>
> ❏ Retirement plans, such as pensions, annuities, IRAs, Keoghs, SEPs, and 401(k)s
>
> ❏ Business interests and business property

- Which assets you can give away to your beneficiaries
- Which of your assets will go through probate
- Whether you should be concerned about minimizing the number of assets that will go through probate (Chapter 6 discusses probate in detail.)
- The total value of your assets and whether your estate will be subject to federal estate taxes

  If your estate will be subject to taxes, minimizing those taxes should be one of your estate planning goals.

The Asset Inventory Section of the Worksheet

To complete the asset inventory section of the estate worksheet, begin by clearly describing each of the assets you own, either as a 100

FIGURE 2.2
Your Estate Planning Worksheet

ASSET INVENTORY

Description of Asset	Type of Ownership	Percentage of Ownership	Net Value of Your Ownership
1.			
2.			
3.			
4.			
5.			
6.			
7.			

Total Current Value of Assets: $

LIABILITY INVENTORY

Description of Liability			Amount You Owe (Your Share of Liability)
1.			
2.			
3.			
4.			
5.			
6.			
7.			

Total Current Liabilities: $

Total Assets	$
Less	
Total Liabilities	$
Total Value of Estate:	**$**

percent owner or as a partial or joint owner. List personal property of significant value, such as fine jewelry, furniture, and vehicles, as well as real property, which includes raw land, your home, and any other buildings you may own. Also, list any business interest you have as a sole proprietor, partner, or principal in a corporation.

Describing Your Assets

Describe each of the assets you list on the worksheet using words that clearly indicate the item you are referring to. Your executor should not have to guess what you are referring to! Here are some suggestions for how to describe your property:

Checking and savings accounts and cash equivalents. Note the type of account, the account number, and the name and address of the financial institution where the account is located.

Furniture. For furniture of value, including antiques, family heirlooms, or collectible pieces, provide a short but precise description of each item. If a piece of furniture is associated with a particular era or style, such as a Chippendale chair or an art deco table, note that information.

Other household items. You may want to group certain types of items with relatively low value together rather than listing each item individually. For example, "All the cooking and kitchen supplies at (your address)" or "All the hand tools and electric tools at (your address)."

Artwork. Describe the subject as well as the artist and the particular era or style of any significant paintings, sculptures, or other artwork you may own. Miscellaneous, less important artwork can be identified with a single description, such as "All the paintings and other artwork at (your address)."

Clothing. List furs, expensive designer clothes, or significant items of vintage clothing separately. Describe them in as much detail as possible, including, when applicable, the name of the designer and the particular style and/or era of an item. Less valuable clothing can be grouped together such as "All the items of female (or male) clothing at (your address)."

Collections. If you own a significant collection of stamps, coins, books, dolls, antique pens or autographs, salt and pepper shakers, and so on, describe it briefly. Include the number of items in the collection and the era of those items when applicable, such as "salt and pepper shakers from the 1920s and 1930s" or "antique china dolls from the 19th century."

Jewelry. List each piece of fine jewelry you may own. Do the same for any family heirloom jewelry items. Specify what the item is made of—gold, silver, types of stones—and the style and era of the piece. If you own a collection of good quality, collectible costume jewelry, you may want to list it as a single item—"All the costume jewelry at (your address)." However, if any of the items can be considered antiques of value, list them separately.

Vehicles. List each vehicle separately. Note its color, make and model, manufacturer, year of manufacture, license number, and vehicle identification number (VIN).

Stocks and mutual funds. For each investment, include the name of the company or name of the fund, number of shares you own, relevant CUSIP number, relevant account number, and the name of the brokerage company that is serving the account.

Bonds. Note the name of the relevant company or government entity, cost of each bond purchased, and the date purchased.

Life insurance policies. For each policy, indicate the policy number, the name of the company that issued the policy, and the name of the policy beneficiary or beneficiaries.

Retirement plans. Note the type of plan, the applicable account number if any, and the company that is administering the plan.

Business interests. If you own an interest in a business, specify the type of business—partnership, corporation, sole proprietorship—and note your share of the business. (If your business is a sole proprietorship, you own 100 percent of it.) If you have an interest in a corporation, indicate the number of shares you own; also, indicate the name and location of the business.

Land and buildings, including your home. List the complete address of each piece of property you own. If you own raw land without a specific address, indicate the number of acres you own and their approximate location, including the nearest town or city and the county where the acreage is located. If you own a second home, such as a lake or ski house, and you intend to leave both the home and its furnishings to a beneficiary, include the home's furnishings in your description of the property—for example, "Vacation home and all furnishings located at (address of your vacation home)."

Type of Ownership

Indicate how you own each of the assets on your worksheet so that you know what you can and cannot give away. As a quick review, you may own 100 percent of an asset or you may own an asset as a *joint tenant with right of survivorship,* as a *tenant by the entirety,* or as a *tenant in common.* In addition, the assets you own are either separate or community property. For a more complete review of your legal ownership options, return to Chapter 1. To save time and space when completing this section of the worksheet, you may want to abbreviate each type of ownership. For example:

Joint tenant with right of survivorship	J.T.W.R.O.S.
Tenant by the entirety	T.E.
Tenant in common	T.C.
Community property	C.P.
Separate property	S.P.

Don't forget that you cannot use your will to transfer assets like life insurance policy benefits, the benefits from an employee retirement plan, or the funds in an IRA or Keogh because you designated the beneficiaries for those assets when you set them up. Therefore, use the abbreviation D.B. (designated beneficiary) in the "Type of Ownership" column when you record one of these assets on your worksheet.

Percentage of Your Ownership

In the column titled "Percentage of Your Ownership" indicate the percentage of each asset that you own. For example, if you own an asset by yourself, that figure will be 100 percent. The percentage will be smaller if you own the asset with one or more persons.

Net Value of Your Ownership

In the worksheet's final column, record the current market value of each asset you have listed. In most instances, current market value is what you could sell the asset for today, not what you bought it for. However, in the case of a bank account, current market value is simply the amount of money in the account.

You should be able to determine the market value of an employee benefit plan, IRA, Keogh, brokerage account, or the like by calling the plan administrator or the company with whom you maintain each investment. The current value should also be indicated on the periodic statements you receive for each investment. If you monitor your investments online, you can also determine their market values by going to the Web site where you maintain your investment information.

If you are unsure of the value of any antiques, artwork, or collectibles you may own, consider having it professionally appraised, especially if you feel that the asset's value is significant. An appraisal helps guard against overvaluing or undervaluing an asset. The appraiser you use should have specific experience appraising the particular type of asset you want valued.

If you own a business or have an interest in one, you may want to consult an experienced certified public accountant to determine the value of your share. As an overview, however, if your business is a sole proprietorship, its value is the dollar amount you could sell the business for. If you're in a partnership or a limited liability corporation, the value of your share could be how much you would be compensated by the business if you were to retire from it or your share of the business's liquidation value. If you have an interest in a closely held corporation, the value of your share of the business and of any buyout agreements that may be in effect need to be considered. If the corporation is publicly held, the value of your business interest depends on the number of shares of the business you own and its current stock price.

Don't worry if some of your asset valuations are approximations. Unless you pull numbers out of thin air, reasonably approximate valuations should not create problems.

> ## HOT TIP
>
> If you're a business owner, issues like the potential impact of your death on the business's ability to continue functioning as a going concern and how you will be compensated at retirement for your share of the business affect the value of your interest.

The Liability Inventory Section of the Worksheet

Your liabilities, or debts, may include outstanding bank or personal loans you're obligated to pay, credit card debt, property liens, debts to the IRS and other taxing entities, outstanding court judgments rendered against you, and any past-due child support or alimony you may be obligated to pay. Don't worry about periodic small obligations like your monthly utility and phone bills.

Your liabilities may also include your share of any outstanding debts related to an asset you may own with others. For example, let's assume you own a beach house with two friends as joint tenants and the market value of the house is $90,000. If the balance on the beach house mortgage is $30,000 and you and your co-owners also owe $5,000 in back taxes, your share of the total debt associated with that asset is $11,667 because you have a one-third interest in the property.

When you complete the liability section of your worksheet, be sure to include the total amount you owe for each debt and relevant account numbers as well as the names and addresses of the companies, government agencies, or individuals to whom you owe the money.

The Estimated Net Value of Your Estate

To determine the estimated net value of your estate, add together the values of all the assets on your worksheet and then subtract from that number the total value of the liabilities listed on the worksheet. If you are determining the net value of your estate in 2001, you do not need to worry about federal estate taxes if its value is $675,000 or less, although state estate taxes may be a concern for some of you. However, as you learned in the previous chapter, President Bush signed into law a bill that gradually increases the estate tax threshold, ends the estate tax for one year, and then reestablishes it the next year. The threshold increases stop in 2009, at which time only estates worth more than $3.5 million will be liable for federal estate taxes. The estate tax is repealed for 2010 and reinstated in 2011. If estate taxes are a concern for you, be sure to consult with an estate planning attorney about what you can do to reduce the size of your taxable estate.

Review and update your estate planning worksheet on a regular basis. During your lifetime, you will probably gain and also lose or sell assets. Also, the value of your assets is likely to appreciate or depreciate. In addition, you may take on new debt or pay off existing debt. Your estate planning worksheet should reflect each change because a change may affect your net worth as well as the kind of estate planning you should do.

H O T   T I P

Everything Your Heirs Need to Know, by David S. Magee and John Ventura (Dearborn, 1999), is a personal recordkeeping organizer. It educates you about the kinds of information you should record and save in order to make it easier for your family and executor after your death and provides you with places to write down that information. The information relates to your assets and debts, family history, and final wishes. It also provides you with spaces for noting the location of important documents your executor and family will need when you die.

3

Selecting Your Executor and Beneficiaries

When you write your will, you have a minimum of three critical decisions to make:

1. Who to name as executor of your estate
2. To whom to leave your property—that is, your beneficiaries
3. What to give to each of your beneficiaries

This chapter helps you make all three decisions. It explains the role and duties of an executor and the factors to consider when you are choosing one and it reviews the issues to consider when you make decisions regarding your beneficiaries.

What Is an Executor?

An executor is the person you name in your will to act as legal representative of your estate after you die. Your executor works with the probate court to carry out a minimum of five key tasks for your estate:

1. Locate your will
2. Inventory and value your assets
3. Pay all legitimate claims against your estate
4. Pay any taxes your estate may owe
5. Distribute your assets to your beneficiaries

A blast aboard a navy ship during World War I almost ended the film career of a person who would be one of Hollywood's most famous and talented actors: Humphrey Bogart. The young son of a doctor, Bogart was badly injured, his face scarred and his upper lip partially paralyzed. The tough guy look that resulted served him well in his career. Bogart started his film career portraying killers, but he really made his mark playing tough guys with a tender heart. His most famous role was Rick in *Casablanca,* the guy who let his love go off with another man and then left to fight in World War II. In 1944, Bogart starred in *To Have and Have Not,* the same year that he married Lauren Bacall. They remained married until his death on January 14, 1957.

In preparing his will, Bogart faced the same decision everyone does when writing a will: who should be selected as executor. Most people choose just one executor. However, Bogart picked three! In addition to his wife, he designated a friend and a Los Angeles bank.

A more complete discussion of your executor's responsibilities is found later in the chapter.

Many people choose their spouse as their executor; but if your spouse is in poor health or would be easily overwhelmed with the responsibilities of being an executor, then it's a good idea to choose someone else. For example, an older child, another family member, or a close friend may make a good executor. Before you name anyone as your executor, however, make sure that your choice for the job is willing to accept it and capable of handling the responsibility, particularly if your estate is complex and quite valuable or if you are concerned that there may be problems after your death that could complicate the probate process.

Don't forget to name a substitute or an alternate executor in your will. This person assumes executor duties should your first choice be unable or unwilling to act as executor after you die. This happened in Humphrey Bogart's case. Lauren Bacall Bogart renounced her right to act as executrix of her husband's estate, so an alternate was needed.

Your executor is legally entitled to be paid a fee for acting as your legal representative, which will be paid by your estate. However, you can stipulate in your will that you don't want your executor to receive a fee. Before you do, however, talk it over with the person you want as your executor. She may not want to take on the job unless she is compensated for it. On the other hand, if you and your executor are especially close, she may waive the fee she is entitled to receive.

If your state requires that your executor be bonded, you can waive that requirement in your will. If you do, there will be more money in your estate to go to your beneficiaries because the cost of the bond would have been deducted from it. However, some states require a cash bond if your executor lives out of state.

> ### HOT TIP
>
> If your will is silent on the matter of an executor fee, the probate court will provide for one. Usually the fee will be a percentage of your estate's total value.

Professional Executors

Rather than designating a friend or relative as your executor, you may prefer to hire a professional executor for your estate. Banks and attorneys most often fill that role. However, professional executors charge a substantial amount of money for their services—money that will come out of your estate. Therefore, using a professional executor makes the most sense if your estate is large and complex; if you are concerned

> ### HOT TIP
>
> A professional knows the ins and outs of the probate process, how to use shortcuts, and how to avoid problems. Therefore, he may be able to save your estate money and speed up the probate process.

that your will may be contested; or if you have reason to believe that the terms of your will may trigger conflict among your family members. Choosing a professional executor is also a good idea when there is not anyone in your life who you feel is capable of handling the job.

Coexecutors

It sometimes makes sense to appoint coexecutors for your will rather than a single executor. If your estate is especially large and complex, for example, you may not want all of the responsibilities of executor to fall on the shoulders of just one person. Another circumstance when a coexecutor arrangement may make sense is when your first choice for executor doesn't live close to you. If you pick a coexecutor who lives nearby, he can help the other executor with the day-to-day details of administering your estate. Be aware, however, that a coexecutor arrangement will probably not work if the coexecutors do not like one another or don't work well together. Their interpersonal problems could slow down the probate process.

Some experts suggest that if you choose a professional executor, you name a family member or close friend as coexecutor. The rationale for this suggestion is that having someone work with the professional executor who is attuned to the needs and interests of your family can make the probate process easier on your loved ones.

What to Look For in an Executor

Your executor is responsible for carrying out many important responsibilities on behalf of your estate. Therefore, the person you choose as executor should be conscientious, well organized, fair-minded, and not easily intimidated by lawyers, legal documents, paperwork, or court bureaucracies. It is also a good idea if your executor is trusted and respected by your family and has the time to do the job. By the way, your choice for executor must be a legal adult and a U.S. citizen and cannot be a convicted felon.

There is one additional and very important quality you should look for in an executor—a willingness to do the job. An executor's responsibilities are too important to entrust to someone who does not really want to do it. Therefore, it is a good idea to review those responsibilities with your choice for executor so that you can be certain that she is willing and able to assume them.

H O T   T I P

If you are a business owner, consider choosing an executor who has experience running your particular type of business.

After you die, the court must formally approve your executor. Although it rarely happens, the court will appoint someone to be the executor of your estate if it denies approval.

Duties of an Executor

The following list describes an executor's typical responsibilities when your estate goes through probate:

- Find and review your will
- Initiate the probate process with the probate court
- Notify all interested parties of your death and of the terms of your will
- Identify the assets in your estate that will go through probate and value each of them
- Manage the assets in your estate while the probate process is ongoing, which may include paying bills, depositing money, investing funds, selling some of your assets, and so on
- Pay the legitimate claims of your creditors as well as any taxes your estate may owe, which may require your executor to sell some of the assets in your estate
- Comply with the reporting requirements of the probate court, file the appropriate legal paperwork, and, as appropriate, notify the Social Security Administration, civil service, Department of Veterans Affairs, etc., of your death
- Help defend your estate against any contests to your will, albeit most wills are not contested
- Communicate with your family and any other beneficiaries of your estate about the progress of the probate process
- Make sure that your assets are distributed to your beneficiaries according to the wishes you expressed in your will
- Prepare a final report for the probate court and formally request that the probate process for your estate be ended

---

H O T   T I P

In most states, an executor is personally responsible for all of your estate's tax liabilities to the extent of the estate and for any late tax filings as well.

Before you write your will, understand the specific powers your state gives to executors as well as any restrictions your state may impose on them. If you want, you may use your will to give your executor additional powers as appropriate, assuming those other powers do not violate your state's laws. Among other things, those additional powers might include the right to make real estate transactions on behalf of your estate and the right to borrow money to pay your estate's debts.

When the fabulously wealthy tobacco heiress Doris Duke died, leaving behind a $1.2 billion estate, her estate quickly became tied up in litigation. A New York judge got rid of the two executors named in Duke's final will, one of whom was her butler, Bernard Lafferty. The other was United States Trust Company. The judge claimed that Lafferty was squandering Duke's estate to support "his profligate lifestyle" and that the United States Trust Company had been letting Lafferty get away with it.

Most executors hire an estate attorney to help them through the probate process. However, the cost of this assistance can be expensive and ordinarily is paid by the estate that is being probated. Therefore, it's a good idea to talk with your executor about when legal help would be appropriate. You may also want to suggest a particular lawyer or law firm if you have a preference. However, you cannot require that your executor follow your wishes regarding legal help. In the end, it is up to your executor whether she hires an attorney and, if she does, which attorney she decides to work with.

Depending on the total value of the assets in your probate estate, it may be eligible for a probate process that is less formal, less expensive, and less costly than the traditional probate process, although not every state offers this alternative. Chapter 6 discusses the alternative probate process in greater detail.

HOT TIP

The heirs to your estate can hold your executor personally responsible for diminishing the value of your estate if they can prove that the loss of value is due to the executor's neglect, breach of duties, or deliberate actions.

Given the important service that your executor will perform for you and your family while you are alive, you should do what you can to make your executor's future job as easy as possible. The steps you take ahead of time can also help avoid delays in the probate process and save your estate money. Figure 3.1 suggests some of the things you can do.

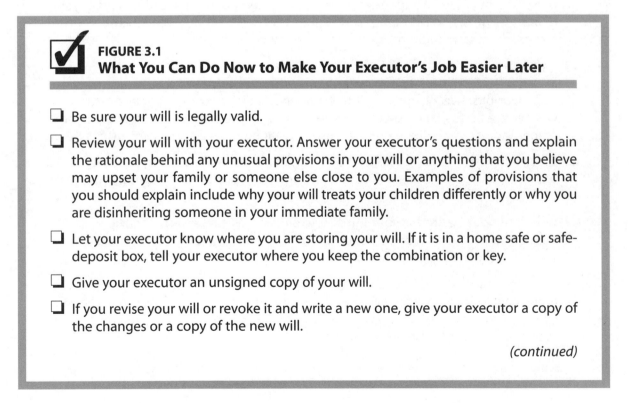

FIGURE 3.1
What You Can Do Now to Make Your Executor's Job Easier Later

❏ Be sure your will is legally valid.

❏ Review your will with your executor. Answer your executor's questions and explain the rationale behind any unusual provisions in your will or anything that you believe may upset your family or someone else close to you. Examples of provisions that you should explain include why your will treats your children differently or why you are disinheriting someone in your immediate family.

❏ Let your executor know where you are storing your will. If it is in a home safe or safe-deposit box, tell your executor where you keep the combination or key.

❏ Give your executor an unsigned copy of your will.

❏ If you revise your will or revoke it and write a new one, give your executor a copy of the changes or a copy of the new will.

(continued)

FIGURE 3.1
What You Can Do Now (continued)

❏ Explicitly state in your will that you expect your executor to hire professionals as needed to help him carry out his duties as executor. This statement will discourage your beneficiaries from complaining if your executor uses the services of an attorney, a CPA, an appraiser, and so on.

❏ Give your executor a copy of your estate planning worksheet. Chapter 2 provides you with a sample worksheet and discusses how to fill it out.

❏ Maintain complete and well-organized records related to your personal finances, property, and investments, and let your executor know where those records are kept. They should include your Social Security number, income tax returns, real estate records, insurance policies, bank accounts, debt documentation, credit card account numbers, records related to your stocks, mutual funds and other investments, ownership papers, and a list of expected death benefits, among other things.

❏ Provide your executor with pertinent information regarding your personal life and family history. This information should include the name of your current spouse, a copy of your marriage certificate, the names of any previous spouses as well as copies of your divorce papers, your birth certificate, your naturalization papers, your military records, and the names and addresses of any children, grandchildren, adoptive children, stepchildren, or children born out of wedlock.

❏ If you own a business or have an interest in one, make sure your executor knows the location of all pertinent records related to the business and what you want done with your business or business interest after you die. If you want your executor to work with a particular employee, be sure to provide your executor with that person's name, address, and phone number. Also, let that employee know your wishes.

❏ Give your executor the names, addresses, and phone numbers of your attorney, CPA, banker, insurance agent, stock broker, and any other professional advisors you work with.

❏ Write out your desire for your burial or cremation as well as any specific arrangements you have made. Be as detailed as possible. Give your executor a copy. Your spouse or unmarried partner should have a copy too.

❏ If you have made arrangements to donate any of your organs after you die, put them in writing. Include the name, address, and phone number of the organization/s you want to donate to. Give a copy of this information to your executor and to your spouse or unmarried partner.

Your Beneficiaries

Your *beneficiaries* are the individuals, organizations, and others to whom you leave your property. They can include your spouse and children, other family members, your unmarried partner, your close friends, your alma mater, a favorite charity, a cherished pet, and so on. Your beneficiaries may or may not be your legal heirs—the relatives who the laws of your state say are entitled to inherit from you if you do not write a will.

Few people who are dying are lucky enough to be able to breathe their last breath with their loved ones around them, but that is exactly how Linda McCartney died of breast cancer in 1998. In a statement given by Paul McCartney at the time of his beloved's wife death, he said that during her final moments of life, he created a last happy vision for her. He told his wife, "It's a fine spring day. We're riding through the woods. The bluebells are out, and the sky is clear blue." Paul went on to say that he had barely gotten his words out when Linda closed her eyes and slipped away.

Obviously, Linda and Paul McCartney shared a great love for one another, and that love was reflected in her choice of beneficiaries. She left her estate to Paul through a trust that she had set up. As long as he lived, he would receive income on a quarterly basis from the trust. Then, the trust principal would go to their four children—Heather Louise, Mary Anna, Stella Nina, and James Louis.

Deciding what you want to leave to each of your beneficiaries may seem like a simple task that you can accomplish quickly. Even so, you should not rush through those decisions if you want to be sure that you leave your assets to those who will benefit from and/or appreciate them the most. Therefore, spend some time thinking about what you own and what you want to accomplish through your will. You should also consider whether any of your decisions may cause problems or conflicts for your beneficiaries and how to deal with them. In addition, you may want to consider the possible consequences of giving a certain asset to a particular person, charity, and so on. To help you think about these issues, ask yourself the following questions:

- Who do I want as my beneficiaries?
- Do any of them have special needs?
- Do I want to treat all of my children the same, or do I have good reasons to treat them differently?
- Do I want to leave everything to my spouse? Will I create tax problems for my spouse if I do that? What can I do now to avoid or minimize those problems?
- Do I want my beneficiaries to have full control of the assets I leave them when I die or as soon as they turn age 18 or 21?
- How can I ensure that the children from my first marriage will receive some of my property when I die?
- Is my spouse a responsible money manager or is she apt to fritter away the money and other assets I leave her and develop financial problems as a result?
- Are any of the gifts I want to leave to a particular beneficiary likely to spark controversy and discord among my heirs, maybe even a contest to my will? What can I do to avoid these problems?
- Can I make someone's life happier and more secure with a special gift?

Your answers to these and any other questions you think of may suggest that you should use other estate planning tools besides a will. For example, if you do not want your daughter to gain full control over the assets you are leaving her once she becomes a legal adult, you may want to place those assets in a trust for her and use the trust document to spell out exactly when your daughter should have control of the assets you place in the trust. (Chapter 4 discusses trusts and other estate planning tools.)

Whenever you designate a beneficiary for a specific asset, you should name an *alternate beneficiary* too. That way, if your primary beneficiary dies, your alternate will get it instead.

Rather than naming a specific beneficiary for each asset, you can leave certain types of assets to a particular category of beneficiary and then define exactly whom you are including within that category. This approach is especially appropriate if your children are beneficiaries of your will. For example, you could leave certain assets to "All of my children" and then name each of your children.

In addition to naming beneficiaries and alternates in your will, you should designate a *residual beneficiary* and an alternate. This beneficiary would receive any and all assets in your estate that you do not leave to a specific beneficiary should you overlook one or more assets when you write your will or forget to revise your will after you acquire a new asset. If you die without transferring a particular asset through your will or by using some other estate planning tool, the probate court decides which of your heirs is legally entitled to that asset.

Humphrey Bogart, a smooth talker all his life, died of throat cancer. In his will, he created the Humphrey Bogart Foundation to fund grants "for medical research with special attention to the field of cancer." The remainder of his estate went to this organization.

HOT TIP

Rather than naming an alternate beneficiary for each asset, you can stipulate in your will that a particular asset should go to your residual beneficiary in the event the asset's primary beneficiary has already died.

HOT TIP

It is not uncommon for a will to direct that all estate-related taxes, fees, and debts be paid out of the residuary estate and that whatever is left over be given to the residual beneficiary.

Naming Your Spouse as a Beneficiary

If you are married and live in a community property state, you and your spouse each own an undivided one-half interest in the total value of all of your community property. Your spouse's one-half interest will be unaffected by your death and vice versa. Therefore, if you want to ensure that your spouse gets your share of the community property when you die, you must specifically name him as the beneficiary of your share in your will. Otherwise, your spouse could end up sharing ownership of your community property with someone else, such as your child or perhaps another relative. Particularly if the asset were an important one, like your home or car, this kind of ownership arrangement could create problems for your spouse. For example, he might want to sell the asset or borrow against it but his co-owner might disagree and prevent your spouse from doing what he wants to with the asset.

H O T   T I P

If your spouse cosigned on a note that is outstanding at the time of your death and your estate does not have enough funds to pay off the debt, the creditor may try to collect the debt from your spouse. In community property states, your spouse may be liable even if he wasn't a cosignator.

If you live in a separate property state, the law says that when you die, your surviving spouse is entitled to a fixed amount of your estate. If you don't leave your spouse at least that amount, your spouse can "take against the will." That means that your spouse can exercise his right to take the fixed amount rather than the amount in your will. Interestingly, in his will, Humphrey Bogart advised his wife not to take against the will because he thought her interests would be better served if she accepted the terms of his will.

Naming Your Minor Children as Beneficiaries

All states limit the amount of property that a minor child can legally own without adult supervision. Usually, the amount is between $2,500 and $5,000. Therefore, if the value of the property you leave your young child in your will is more than your state's maximum, you must designate a property guardian for the child in the will. The property guardian will manage the property on your child's behalf until the child becomes a legal adult. (Chapter 5 tells you more about leaving money and other assets to minor children.)

Naming Charitable Organizations as Beneficiaries

You can use your will to give your assets to a charitable organization. You can indicate that you want the charity to use your gift for a general or a specific purpose. If the organization is an IRS-approved charity, your gift is exempt from federal gift and estate taxes and from those same taxes in most states.

If you include any charities in your will, be sure that you list each organization's complete legal name and exact address. Otherwise, you may unintentionally benefit the wrong organization.

HOT TIP

Some states restrict charitable gift giving in a will. To find out if your state imposes such restrictions, talk to an estate attorney.

Remembering Your Pet

You can remember Fido or Whiskers or some other pet in your will with restrictions. In most states, you cannot give any assets directly to a pet nor can you set up a trust for a pet in the animal's name. However, you can leave money in your will to a family member or friend and stipulate that the funds be used to care for your pet after your death. Another more expensive way to remember your pet is to establish a trust in the name of a friend, family member, or someone else and specify in the trust document what the funds must be used for.

Doris Duke loved animals and donated some of her fortune to the Doris Duke Foundation for the Preservation of Endangered Wildlife. She also used her will to provide for her pet dog. Here is what her will says about the dog: "If I shall be survived by a dog owned by me and residing at my death at my residence known as Falcon's Lair in Beverly Hills, California, I give such dog to the caretaker of such property at my death or, if such caretaker is at any time unwilling or unable to care for such dog, to one of the foundations created under this will or of which I was a member, director, trustee or officer at my death which is caring for other dogs of mine. If I shall be survived by a dog owned by me and located at my death at Falcon's Lair, I give and bequeath the sum of One Hundred Thousand Dollars ($100,000.00) to my Trustees, to be held by them in a separate trust for the benefit of such a dog."

H O T   T I P

Don't leave money in your will to a friend or family member for the care of a pet unless you are sure that the person is willing to assume the responsibility. The same is true if you set up a trust for the care of your pet and want to name a friend or family member as trustee.

Special Messages and Explanations

You can do more with your will than designate who gets what. You can also use your will to leave behind special messages. For example, you might want to let your spouse or child know how much you love him or you might want to tell each of your family members what you most appreciate about them. If you're like most people, you may not have many valuable assets to leave to the important people in your life, so the special messages in your will can serve as your gifts— final expressions of your feelings for them. For some of the people you care about, your message may mean more than any asset you could ever leave them.

You can also make special explanations in your will. This can be a good idea if you are concerned that your will may trigger discord within your family or among your beneficiaries or maybe even generate a will contest. For example, if you do not leave each of your children the same share of your estate, or if you leave a substantial amount of money to someone who is not one of your legal heirs, you can explain why in your will. You should also provide your executor, as well as your beneficiaries and legal heirs if appropriate, with the same explanation before you die.

If the reason you are leaving someone out of your will or are giving one child much less than another involves issues that are negative or potentially embarrassing to the person being left out or receiving less than others, it is probably best not to put the explanation in your will because a will is a public document that anyone can read. Also, you risk having your estate sued for libel if you include something negative or embarrassing to someone in your will. A better approach is to provide the person involved with an explanation while you are still alive. Your executor should get the same explanation.

Giving Options

When you are thinking about what you own and to whom you want to leave your property, remember two things:

1. Certain types of assets will automatically convey to beneficiaries outside your will. For a review of the types of assets you can and cannot transfer to others with your will, return to Chapter 1.
2. In addition to writing a will, you can use other estate planning tools to transfer your assets to your beneficiaries. The next chapter tells you about those other estate planning tools.

4

If You Want to Do More Than Write a Will

Depending on the value of your estate and on your estate planning goals, you may want to do more than write a will. Therefore, this chapter introduces you to other estate planning tools you may want to use. It also explains when and why a particular tool may be appropriate for you and provides an overview of each tool's advantages and disadvantages.

Estate Planning Tools

Understanding the range of tools available to you helps you make informed decisions when you do your estate planning. The following are the estate planning tools this chapter covers:

- Joint ownership of assets
- *Inter vivos* gifts
- Life insurance
- Employee benefits and other retirement plans
- Informal bank trust accounts
- Testamentary and living trusts

Figure 4.1 summarizes the key advantages and disadvantages of each estate planning tool compared with a will. Chapter 9 discusses two other things you should do when you are planning your estate— write a living will and prepare a durable power of attorney.

FIGURE 4.1

Comparing the Advantages and Disadvantages of Key Estate Planning Tools

Will

Advantages

- Easy and relatively inexpensive to prepare
- Allows you to name a personal and a property guardian for a minor child
- Can be modified at any time up to your death

Disadvantages

- Property in a will subject to probate
- A minor automatically receives the asset(s) at 18 or 21, depending on your state. You can get around this drawback, however, by using your will to set up a testamentary trust for the minor and specifying at what age you want the minor to receive that property.
- Probate often time-consuming and expensive

Joint Tenancy

Advantages

- Inexpensive and simple to use
- Avoids probate

Disadvantages

- Lack of full control over an asset you own as a joint tenant
- Gift taxes may be involved in making a solely owned asset a joint asset

Inter Vivos Gift

Advantages

- Helps reduce the size of an estate for probate and tax purposes

Disadvantages

- Lose use of the property you give away

Life Insurance

Advantages

- Safe, secure way to build an estate
- Avoids probate
- No income tax liability associated with benefits
- Good way to provide liquidity for estate

Disadvantages

- No flexibility governing when and how death benefits are paid to the beneficiary(ies) of your policy (You can deal with this disadvantage by making a trust the beneficiary of those proceeds. In the trust document you can spell out when and under what conditions the trust's beneficiary can receive the money.)

Employee Benefits

Advantages
- Death benefits avoid probate

Disadvantages
- No flexibility in how probate benefits are paid to the beneficiary(ies) of your benefits
- Have tax consequences

Informal Bank Trust Accounts

Advantages
- Usually are revocable
- Inexpensive and easy to set up
- Account funds avoid probate

Disadvantages
- No flexibility in how or when account funds are paid to beneficiary

Testamentary Trust

Advantages
- Provides tax advantages
- You can control when trust beneficiary receives trust assets
- Not established until you die

Disadvantages
- Trust assets go through probate before reaching trust

Revocable Living Trust

Advantages
- Avoids probate
- You have control of trust assets while you are alive
- You can be both trustee and beneficiary of the trust
- You can control when a trust beneficiary receives trust assets and income

Disadvantages
- Relatively expensive to set up
- No tax advantages unless you go to the extra expense of combining a revocable living trust with a second trust that is designed to save on estate taxes

Irrevocable Living Trust

Advantages
- Avoids probate
- Provides tax advantages
- You can control when a trust beneficiary receives trust assets and income

Disadvantages
- Relatively expensive to set up
- Once an asset is placed in an irrevocable trust, it can't be removed or changed in any other way

At the time of her death, Doris Duke was one of the wealthiest women in the world. She left behind a very complicated will and estate, and her death also raised many questions about her mental condition at the time she wrote her will, the intentions of the people involved in her life during her last years, as well as the circumstances of her death.

If her will is any indication, Duke was an interesting and unusual person. For example, in addition to creating a $100,000 trust for the "care, feeding, comfort, maintenance and medical treatment" of her dog, she gave her eyes to the Eye Bank for Sight Restoration and asked to be buried at sea.

Another interesting aspect of her will is that Duke listed in it people who owed her money and specifically forgave all but one person's debt. The debt she didn't forgive was the $5 million she loaned to Imelda Marcos, wife of the former president of the Philippines.

Joint Ownership

Owning assets with someone else as joint tenants with right of survivorship is an inexpensive and simple estate planning tool. As explained in Chapter 1, if you and another person own property as joint tenants, your share automatically passes to your co-owner when you die. Therefore, assets owned this way do not need to be included in your will and they do not go through probate.

Spouses frequently own such assets as a home or a bank account as joint tenants. However, you can also own property as a joint tenant with another relative, your unmarried partner, a close friend, or someone else. For example, Humphrey Bogart's will indicates that the home he shared with his wife, Lauren Bacall Bogart, was owned by them as joint tenants. He considered all of their other property to be community property.

Another type of joint ownership very similar to joint tenancy is tenancy by the entirety. This form of ownership, however, is only available to spouses. Real estate and bank accounts are commonly owned as tenants by the entirety.

Before you rush off to make all of your assets joint assets with one of your beneficiaries as your co-owner, you should be aware of the potential drawbacks to this form of ownership that are described below.

- *You don't have full control over a joint asset.* Therefore, you can't sell the asset if your co-owner balks, although your co-owner could give away her share or even lose it as the result of a court judgment against her. For example, one of your co-owner's creditors could come after her share of your joint asset to collect on a past-due debt. In fact, it's possible that you could end up owning a joint asset with someone you don't know should your co-owner lose her share in a collection action or give her share away.

- *If you no longer want to own an asset as a joint tenant, it can be extremely difficult, if not impossible, to change the nature of your ownership.*

- *If you change an asset that you own by yourself into a joint asset by giving a share of the asset to someone else, it may be viewed as an* inter vivos *gift.* Depending on the value of the share, your estate may be subject to a federal gift tax. The gift tax does not apply, however, if you give your share to your spouse.

- *Some states freeze the funds in a joint bank account after a joint account holder dies.* To regain access to the account, the other account owner must present certain legal documents. If the other account owner is your surviving spouse and if he needs the account funds to pay bills and/or to help pay your funeral and burial expenses, the delay created by having to locate and present those documents could be a hardship for your spouse.

- *Joint ownership can make it difficult for a spouse to become eligible for Medicaid.* This can be a serious problem if a spouse needs long-term care and does not have private long-term care insurance. If paying for long-term care insurance may be an issue for you or your spouse in the near future, consult with an attorney who is familiar with elder law and the rules of Medicaid before you make an asset a joint asset with your spouse or end a joint ownership arrangement. If you are in your late 50s or early 60s, you may also want to look into purchasing long-term care insurance. Such insurance is too expensive to buy at an earlier age, although the price of such policies has been coming down.

- *Joint ownership can create tax problems for husbands and wives with substantial estates.* An estate planning attorney can advise you how to deal with such problems.

Inter Vivos Gifts

Many people give away their assets while they are still alive. Gifts to beneficiaries that are made this way are called *inter vivos* gifts. You can make a trust the recipient of an *inter vivos* gift.

You may want to make *inter vivos* gifts for a variety of reasons, including:

- To experience the pleasure of giving while you are alive and of knowing how much the recipients of your gifts benefit from and appreciate them
- To minimize the value of the assets in your estate that will go through probate so that the probate process can be completed more quickly or so that your estate can qualify for an alternative probate process that may be available in your state. This alternative is faster and less expensive than the traditional probate process.
- To minimize the size of your taxable estate because the asset you give away as an *inter vivos* gift is no longer part of your estate and therefore not liable for estate taxes

Federal law allows you to give up to $10,000 in money or other assets each year to as many individuals or charities as you want without triggering a gift tax, assuming your *inter vivos* gifts meet certain criteria. If you and your spouse make the *inter vivos* gifts together, you can give a total of $20,000 to each beneficiary each year without concern about the tax implications of your gifts.

To be considered an *inter vivos* gift, an asset must be

- a present interest in something. Giving someone a future interest in an asset you own is not an *inter vivos* gift.
- irrevocable. In other words, you cannot take the gift back. If you do, the gift no longer provides you with tax benefits.
- a completed gift. You must give up all ownership rights to the asset and cannot control it in any way.

To make sure that an *inter vivos* gift provides you with the tax benefits you anticipate, you must be sure to take care of all the necessary legal paperwork. For example, if you give away real property or a car, you must change the name of the owner on all the ownership documents, give them to the new owner, and file the required paperwork with the courts in the new owner's name. If the gift is intangible, such as stocks, bonds, or bank accounts, you must provide the new owner with the investment certificates or passbooks for the accounts and make sure that the new owner's name is on all related documents.

HOT TIP

If you make an *inter vivos* gift of real estate, you may need to get the property appraised to confirm that it is in fact worth $10,000 or less to avoid paying a gift tax.

HOT TIP

A gift will not qualify for tax benefits if you change the title paperwork into the new owner's name but keep the new title rather than giving it to the person whose name is now on that document. Under those circumstances, the gift is not a completed gift as you still have the title document.

When you write your will, you may want to specify that the value of any *inter vivos* gifts you have already given to any of your beneficiaries should not be treated as an advance on what you've left them in your will. If you don't stipulate this, it is possible that your beneficiaries will not receive all that you intend for them to have through your will. This same advice also applies to trusts and *inter vivos* gifts.

Life Insurance

Purchasing a life insurance policy is a very safe way to build an asset over time to provide for a beneficiary or to provide your executor with the money she may need to help pay your estate's probate costs, debts, and taxes.

So long as the beneficiary of your life insurance policy is not your estate, the policy proceeds will not go through probate when you die. Therefore, they will be available immediately after your death. However, if your estate is the policy beneficiary, the insurance proceeds will be probated.

A potential, second drawback of making your estate the beneficiary of a life insurance policy is that the proceeds will be subject to the claims of any creditors you may owe money to at the time of your death. However, in most states the proceeds will be protected from those claims if you make the policy payable to your spouse, a dependent, or to a trust for the benefit of someone else. Your estate attorney can tell you how your state treats life insurance proceeds.

H O T   T I P

The proceeds from your life insurance policy may be exempt from your state's inheritance tax.

The main disadvantage of using an insurance policy as an estate planning tool is its lack of flexibility. For example, as the policyholder, you cannot specify when the beneficiary of your policy should receive the policy proceeds or how the proceeds will be paid—lump sum, in a series of payments, and so on. Everything is spelled out in the insurance policy.

This lack of flexibility could be a problem if the value of the policy death benefits is substantial and especially if your beneficiary is a poor money manager. The worst-case scenario is that your beneficiary may squander the policy proceeds, leaving him without enough income to live on.

HOT TIP

You can get around an insurance policy's lack of flexibility by placing the policy in a trust. The proceeds will be held by the trust, and you can dictate in the trust paperwork how you want the money paid out to the trust beneficiary.

Employee Benefits

Employee benefits and individual retirement accounts (IRAs) are common estate planning tools. Employee benefits include pension plans, 401(k)s, annuities, profit-sharing plans, stock options, bonuses, and so on.

Typically, employee benefits plans and IRAs provide you with retirement income while you're alive and also provide benefits to your designated beneficiary after you die. To find out how and when the benefits will be paid out, read the documentation related to your employee benefits or IRA, or talk with the plan administrator.

Having the death benefits from your employee benefits plan or IRA paid to a beneficiary over time in a series of periodic payments, like an annuity, can be a good way to help that person pay her living expenses. Generally, the death benefits do not go through probate unless you name your estate as beneficiary.

The major drawback of using an employee benefits plan or IRA as an estate planning tool is that they both lack flexibility. Like a life insurance policy, you have no control over how and when your beneficiary will receive the death benefits from those assets. However, as with insurance, you can eliminate this drawback by setting up a trust to receive the benefits.

Informal Bank Trusts

Payable-on-death (POD) accounts and Totten trusts are informal bank trusts. They are inexpensive and easy-to-establish estate planning tools. They are also practical alternatives to a formal trust for people with modest estates. The funds in these types of accounts do not go through probate.

You can establish an informal bank trust simply by opening an account in your name at a bank or at another authorized financial institution, such as a brokerage house, and designating an account beneficiary. You and your spouse or you and someone else can establish an informal trust together. While you are alive, you have use of the account funds. When you die, anything left in the account passes directly to the account beneficiary.

HOT TIP

You can convert your existing bank account into an informal trust by filling out the appropriate paperwork at your bank. You can do the same thing with a certificate of deposit or money market account.

The primary disadvantage of an informal trust account is that you have no control over how and when the funds in the account are paid to your beneficiary. After you die, all of the account funds go straight to the account beneficiary. Therefore, you may only want to use an informal trust to transfer small amounts of funds.

Most states permit informal trusts, but some states place limits on them. You can find out how your state treats them by speaking with the appropriate person at your financial institution or with your estate planning attorney.

HOT TIP

In some states the probate court can take the funds in an informal trust account to pay estate-related taxes, fees, and any debts you owe to your creditors when there is not enough money in your estate to cover them.

Trusts

A trust is a legal entity for holding assets you have earmarked for a beneficiary. Like a corporation, a trust has its own legal identity that is totally separate from your's.

A trust is the most flexible of all estate planning tools, which is one of the key explanations for why trusts are so popular and so useful. You can set up a trust to do just about anything as long as the trust's purpose doesn't conflict with the laws of your state and doesn't promote anything that would be considered against public policy.

More than any other estate planning tool, a trust gives you control over the assets you leave to a beneficiary, even after you die. For example, you can stipulate exactly when and under what conditions the beneficiary of a trust can receive the trust assets. When you make those decisions, you take into account a beneficiary's financial needs, age, maturity, physical or mental limitations, money management abilities, and so on. Figure 4.2 highlights some of the more common types of trusts.

The two basic types of trusts are *testamentary trusts* and *living trusts.* A testamentary trust is relatively easy and inexpensive to set up. It is created according to the directions you lay out in your will. Prior to your death, a testamentary trust exists on paper only—in your will—and no assets are transferred into it. After you die, however, the trust comes into existence and assets you've earmarked for the trust are transferred into it to be distributed to the trust beneficiary(ies).

As its name implies, you set up a living trust, or *inter vivos* trust, while you are still alive. That is a key difference between a testamentary and a living trust. After you set up a living trust, you transfer to it ownership of assets you want to go to the trust's beneficiary(ies). The trustee you designate manages those assets. See Figure 4.3.

HOT TIP

Depending on your state, a living trust may damage your eligibility to receive Medicaid benefits. Medicaid is a federal-state program that provides health benefits for low-income and elderly people. Many people use Medicaid to help them pay for long-term care when they cannot continue living at home.

FIGURE 4.2
Examples of Common Types of Trusts

There are many different types of trusts. Some have a very general purpose while others have a much more narrow purpose. To give you a feel for the variety of types of trusts, listed here are some of the more common.

- *Insurance trusts* are created to purchase life insurance and to provide tax benefits.

- *Spendthrift trusts* are established to manage funds for a beneficiary you feel does not have the ability to manage the money and other property you leave to him or her. For example, the person could be a poor money manager, developmentally challenged, or mentally ill.

- *Bypass trusts* are used in combination with the unlimited marital deduction to allow one spouse to provide for the other spouse without concern for estate taxes when there is a substantial estate involved.

- *Qualified terminable interest property (QTIP) trusts* can help you provide for your children by a previous spouse and for your current spouse too. Your current spouse benefits from the trust assets while she is alive, but after her death the remaining assets go to the children from your previous marriage.

- *Generation-skipping trusts* let you transfer up to $1 million in assets (up to $2 million if you and your spouse make the transfer) to your grandchildren. The parents of those children can use the trust income and principal to pay for the children's care—housing, education, and medical care, for example. The new tax legislation signed by President Bush provides for increases in the value of assets that can be transferred by a generation-skipping trust. The increases mirror the increases in the estate tax exemption.

- *Charitable trusts* can be set up to make regular gifts to a charity and to provide tax benefits.

- *Standby trusts* are set up while you are alive but are not funded until your death. They may be funded by the proceeds from your life insurance policy or retirement benefits, among other things. The assets in standby trusts do not go through probate. They can also provide tax benefits.

- *Grantor-retained annuity trusts* are irrevocable trusts commonly used to transfer ownership of a closely held business. They allow the current owner to continue receiving income from the business and to control the business.

- *Medicaid-qualifying trusts* can help you become eligible for nursing home care under the federal Medicaid program and maintain most of the value of your estate at the same time. Therefore, this kind of trust helps you keep much of what you own and then pass it on to your beneficiaries.

FIGURE 4.3
Advantages and Disadvantages of a Revocable Living Trust

Don't set up a revocable living trust until you understand its pros and cons. You need this information to determine if you really need one.

Advantages

- It gives you maximum flexibility and control regarding when and under what conditions your beneficiary can receive the trust assets.

- The trust assets don't go through probate.

- You can be both trustee and beneficiary of a living trust, which means you can control, as well as benefit from, the trust assets.

- It is harder for disgruntled heirs to challenge a living trust compared to challenging a will.

Disadvantages

- You still need to write a will.

- A living trust is a relatively expensive estate planning tool compared with other tools.

- A living trust does not protect your estate from your creditors.

- It provides no income or estate tax advantages, although it can be combined with other kinds of trusts to save on estate taxes.

A living trust is totally separate from your will. That is another key distinction between a testamentary and a living trust. You create a living trust outside your will.

A living trust can be either revocable or irrevocable. Most living trusts are revocable even though revocable trusts do not provide any estate tax advantages. However, the assets that you place in a living trust don't go through probate. In other words, a living trust helps reduce your estate's potential probate costs and your beneficiary receives the trust assets faster than if you had left them to her in your will.

No matter what kind of trust you set up, you create a trust by preparing a trust agreement. This document states the purpose of the trust, spells out the trust's key details including those listed in Figure 4.4, and states any special instructions or requirements you may have for the trustee and for the trust beneficiary.

H O T   T I P

When you set up a revocable living trust, while you are alive, the IRS treats the assets that you place in it just like any other property you may own. Therefore any money the trust assets may make or lose must be reflected on your income tax return, not on a separate return for the trust. When you die, however, the trust must begin filing its own tax returns. Also, you do not have to worry about gift taxes when you transfer assets to the trust since you still control them. Gift taxes apply only to *inter vivos* gifts.

FIGURE 4.4
Key Details of a Trust Agreement

- Purpose of the trust

- Name(s) of the trust's beneficiary(ies)

- Name of the trustee

- Specific powers and responsibilities you give the trustee. You can also use the trust agreement to prohibit the trustee from doing certain things.

- In general terms, your expectations regarding how the trustee should manage the trust's assets. For example, you can instruct the trustee to manage the assets in a manner that conserves the trust principal or to manage them aggressively to maximize the income the assets can produce.

- What you want done with any income the trust may generate—reinvest the income or distribute it to the trust's beneficiary(ies). You can also tie receipt of that income to stated milestones in the life of the beneficiary(ies) or state that the income can be used only for a particular purpose—to pay for a college education, for example.

- When you want your beneficiary(ies) to take full control of the assets in the trust, at which time the trustee's responsibilities will end.

As noted in Chapter 3, Humphrey Bogart, the tough guy in the movie *Casablanca,* was a U.S. Navy veteran who loved the sea and loved to sail. Even though he wanted his ashes scattered at sea, the law at the time would not allow it. Instead, a model of his sailboat, the *Santana,* was displayed at his funeral rather than a coffin.

Bogart was 44 when he met Lauren Bacall, a young actress who filmed the movie *To Have and Have Not* with him. She was just 19. When Bogart died, he left everything to Bacall and their two children, Stephen and Leslie, in trusts. He wanted to make sure all of them were taken care of. He wanted his beloved wife to "live lavishly through the uncertainties of the many years I hope her life will continue in the event of my decease."

HOT TIP

If you want a living trust to be revocable, make its revocability explicit in the trust document.

The Flexibility of a Trust

To illustrate just how flexible a trust can be, here are some estate planning goals and an explanation of how trusts can help you accomplish each of them:

- *Goal: You want to provide for your child's financial needs in the event you and your spouse both die while the child is still a minor and you want to ensure that the money and other assets you leave your child will be managed to maximize their value.* If you place the assets you have earmarked for your child in a trust, you can stipulate how you want the trustee to manage and use them on your child's behalf. The trustee will not be constrained by the legal restrictions and requirements that states place on property guardians.

- *Goal: You plan on leaving your teenage grandchildren a substantial amount of money, but you don't want them to have access to that money as soon as they become legal adults because you don't think they will be mature enough at that age to manage the money wisely.* When you set up a trust for your grandchildren, you can stipulate when they will have control of the money and how much of the trust income, if any, they will receive each year up to that point. Elvis Presley created a trust for his daughter, Lisa Marie Presley. When Lisa Marie turned 25 years old, the trust ended and she got all of the assets that had been placed in it.

- *Goal: Your child is mentally handicapped and can neither earn an income nor manage her money. Therefore, you want to be sure that she will be well cared for after you die.* You can establish a trust for your daughter without jeopardizing any government benefits she is already receiving or may be eligible for.

- *Goal: You are worried that your much younger and free-spending spouse will quickly squander everything you leave to her at your death.* You can set up a trust that prevents her from ever having unfettered access to the assets you place in the trust. Instead, the person you name as trustee will manage the assets for your surviving spouse and provide her with a regular income from the trust. The trustee can also fund from the trust assets special needs and requests your spouse may have, assuming you give the trustee that power in the trust paperwork.

- *Goal: Your health is failing and you are concerned that in the not too distant future you may no longer be able to manage your own finances.* You can set up a trust, name yourself as both trustee and beneficiary, and designate a cotrustee as well. When you are no longer able to act as trustee, your cotrustee will take over, managing the trust assets according to the instructions you have spelled out in the trust document.

- *Goal: You own real estate in multiple states and are worried that your executor will have to deal with the probate process in each state.* You can get around this problem if you place your real estate in a trust.

- *Goal: You want to leave your vacation home to your three children so they can all continue to enjoy it after you die, but you are worried that they may end up in conflicts over its use.* With a trust, you can leave the vacation home to all of your children and dictate rules of use for it.

- *Goal: You plan on leaving all of your assets to your current spouse, but you want to be sure that a share of those assets will go to the children from your previous marriage after she dies.* You can address this concern with a trust.
- *Goal: You want to reduce your estate taxes or minimize the amount of your estate that must go through probate.* Again, a trust is the answer.

Doris Duke's will is a good example of the many ways that trusts can be used. She created the Doris Duke Foundation for the Preservation of Endangered Species of All Kinds, Both Flora and Fauna, from Becoming Extinct and gave her two camels, two horses, and donkey to the foundation. Duke also created the Doris Duke Charitable Foundation. This trust had several purposes, including contributing to the assistance of actors, dancers, singers, musicians, and other artists of the entertainment world in fulfilling their ambitions and providing opportunities for the public presentation of their arts and talents; preserving wildlife; promoting medical research to cure major diseases; and helping any organization actively promoting antivivisectionism. Perhaps Duke's most unusual trust was the one she established to benefit her dog.

HOT TIP

To encourage your beneficiary to do or not do something, you can include one or more incentive clauses in the trust you set up. For example, your trust can provide that if the trust beneficiary earns X amount of money during a given period of time, she will receive X amount of money from the trust.

More about Living Trusts

Given the time and expense involved in setting up a living trust, don't establish one until you have weighed its benefits versus its costs and then compared them to the costs and benefits of other estate planning tools available to you. When you make this analysis and comparison, bear in mind your estate planning goals. You may conclude that there are easier and less expensive ways to achieve those goals. For example, if one of your goals is to avoid the expense of probate, compare the cost of setting up a living trust and transferring assets into the trust with the costs your estate would incur if those assets were to go through probate. Remember that most states offer modestly sized estates a cheaper and faster alternative to the formal probate process. If your estate qualifies for this alternative, there may be no need for you to incur the costs of setting up a living trust.

Consult with an estate planning attorney before you set up a living trust. The attorney can help you determine whether you really need one and can also provide you with advice and information that may save you time and money if you do decide to establish a living trust. In fact, it is unwise to establish either a living trust or a testamentary trust without a lawyer's assistance. Trusts can be complicated to establish and if you don't do everything right, the trust will not help you accomplish your estate planning goals. Also, the attorney can help you coordinate the trust with the rest of your estate planning.

Assets commonly placed in a living trust include wholly owned stocks, bonds, life insurance, and real estate. You cannot place a retirement account in a living trust, but you can designate a living trust as the beneficiary of that account, even though the living trust becomes liable for income taxes if you do. An individual who is the beneficiary of a retirement account may have to pay income taxes on the money in the account as well, but the beneficiary and the IRS can probably negotiate a plan for paying the taxes over time if paying them in full is a problem. A living trust can't do that.

HOT TIP

Although there are many advantages to setting up a living trust, having one does not eliminate the need for you to write a will. See Figure 4.5 for more on why you still need a will.

The Trustee

When you set up a trust, you must designate someone to serve as its trustee. You may choose a family member, a close friend, a lawyer, a bank trust department, or a trust company as trustee. Be sure to name

---

FIGURE 4.5
If You've Got a Living Trust, Why Have a Will?

If you set up a living trust, you still need a will, even if you place most of your assets in the trust. You need a will to do the following:

- Transfer any property you may have overlooked when you set up the trust.

- Transfer property you acquired after you set up the living trust and never placed in the trust.

- Name a personal and a property guardian for your minor child.

---

an alternate or a successor trustee in case your first choice for trustee is unable to carry out the duties when the time comes.

The trustee will manage the assets you place in the trust according to the instructions you set out in the trust agreement on behalf of the trust's beneficiary. Therefore, your choice for trustee should be someone with good financial sense and sound judgment and someone you have confidence in. For example, if you establish a trust to provide for your spouse or your mentally challenged child after you die, the trustee may have responsibility for managing the assets in the trust for many years and could therefore have a direct effect on the long-term financial well-being of your loved one.

Trustees are entitled to be compensated for their services. Usually they receive a flat fee or a fee that is a percentage of the value of the assets in the trust they are managing. The fee arrangement depends on the state where the trust is located. Although a nonprofessional trustee may waive the fee, a professional trustee will not.

HOT TIP

If a trustee's responsibilities will continue for many years, you may want to consider appointing a professional trustee to manage the trust assets. A professional can help ensure a consistent quality of trust asset management over the years.

When you set up a living trust, legal ownership of the assets you place in it are transferred to the trust. In other words, you no longer own them. However, in some states, you can "have your cake and eat it too" by making yourself the trustee. In most states, you can also name yourself as beneficiary of the trustee. By wearing both hats, you can maintain control of the trust assets while you are alive, use them, and also benefit from them. This option is an important potential advantage of a living trust.

Transferring ownership of assets to a trust can be a time-consuming process and expensive too. Among other things, the banks and title companies involved in the transfer process may want to review your trust agreement to confirm that you have given the trustee sufficient power to manage the trust assets. Many people use attorneys to help them with the ownership transfer process, but if money is a concern, you can handle the transfers yourself.

H O T   T I P

If you name yourself as trustee of a living trust, be sure to appoint a successor or a cotrustee, depending on the purpose of the trust. This person will take over if you are no longer able to manage the trust for some reason, or if you die.

Some Living Trusts Are Scams

It's time for a note of caution about living trusts. Beware of living trust fraud. It is not uncommon. Unscrupulous living trust salespersons are in the business of convincing people that they need a living trust and that they can substitute one for a will. Often they use misinformation and scare tactics to make their sale. For example, a typical sales pitch warns consumers that probate will eat up their hard-earned assets and that it could be years before their beneficiaries would ever receive what they leave them in their wills. This message may be conveyed through a living trust seminar, direct mail, newspaper ads, and even door-to-door sales. Sadly, the people who fall for living trust scams often die with neither a legally valid trust nor a will. Furthermore, trusts sold this way tend to be nothing more than boilerplate forms that are not tailored to the specific needs of the people who purchase them. Older people are particular targets of living trust salespeople.

Other businesses sell living trust do-it-yourself kits. Consumers who send money for these kits often end up with nothing to show for their money.

Figure 4.6 summarizes the telltale signs of a living trust scam.

 FIGURE 4.6
Seven Tips for Spotting a Living Trust Scam

1. Avoid a fill-in-the-blanks or preprinted living trust form. Your living trust should be drafted to reflect your particular financial situation, the needs of your beneficiaries, your estate planning goals, and the laws of your state. A fill-in-the-blanks living trust form may not allow you to do that.

2. Steer clear of living trust salespeople who try to sell you a living trust over the phone, by mail, at a seminar, or though a door-to-door solicitation. No matter what they claim their credentials are, don't give them any money or sign any of their paperwork!

3. Don't work with a living trust salesperson, financial planner, attorney, or the like who describes living trusts as panaceas that can resolve all of your estate planning issues—reduce your estate taxes, avoid probate, save you money, and protect your estate from creditors. Living trusts are wonderful estate planning tools but they can't do everything.

4. Avoid salespeople who use fear and/or distrust of attorneys as their rationale for why you need a living trust.

5. Don't work with living trust salespeople who play up all of the negatives associated with the probate process to convince you to purchase a living trust. They are probably exaggerating the downside of probate.

6. If you're approached by someone wanting to sell you a living trust, check out the company the salesperson works for before you pay any money or sign any paperwork related to the trust. Among other things, contact the consumer protection division of your state attorney general's office and your local better business bureau to find out whether they have complaints on file about the company.

7. Don't purchase a living trust without asking an estate attorney to review the living trust paperwork first.

HOT TIP

If someone tries to sell you a living trust, ask if the seller is an attorney. Some states permit only attorneys to sell living trusts. Even if your state does not have this restriction, to protect yourself you should purchase your living trust from an estate planning attorney.

Estate Planning for Business Owners

If you are a business owner, you have special estate planning issues to consider. Answering the following questions can help you determine which issues you face and how best to deal with them. In part, which issues relate to your situation depend on the legal structure of your business.

- What do you want to have happen to your business after you die? Your options include sell it, pass it on to one or more of your family members to own and run, or liquidate the assets.
- If you want your business to continue as a source of income for your beneficiaries, who will own it and who will manage it?
- How will you transfer ownership of your business to the new owners?
- Do you have a succession plan in place?
- What is the value of your business? How should its value be determined?
- Do you want your business to go through probate? If not, what can you do to protect it from that process?
- How will your estate taxes be paid? If you are like many people, your business is your most valuable asset, but without appropriate tax planning, your family could be forced to sell your business or liquidate its assets to pay your estate taxes. (This issue is addressed later in this chapter.)
- If you want your business sold or liquidated after you die, what should you do now to prepare for that transaction?

If you are a business owner, hire an estate planning attorney who has specific experience working with businesses. The rest of this chapter covers in greater detail some of the key issues your estate planning should address. Having this information better prepares you to work effectively with your estate planning attorney.

How Your Business's Legal Structure Affects Estate Planning

If your business is a sole proprietorship, you may be its only employee. Therefore, when you die, your business will probably die too, for its viability is totally dependent on your skills, knowledge, and business contacts.

You have several options regarding the future of your sole proprietorship when you do your estate planning. One option is to find someone else to take over your business. That person could be one of your children, your spouse, a friend, another business owner, or even a stranger. Second, if your business has substantial assets and if its client list is valuable, you could sell the business. A third option is to arrange for the liquidation or sale of your business assets after you die. This final option is viable only if your business owns substantial assets that would be of value to someone else.

When your business is a partnership, you share its ownership with one or more partners. Therefore, you can't decide by yourself what will happen to your share of the business after you die and how much your share is worth. Those are decisions you must share with your partners. In fact, they may be addressed in the partnership agreement you drew up when you established the business.

If your business is incorporated and you do not own 100 percent of the corporation's shares, like a partnership, what will happen to those shares when you die and what they are worth are not up to you. A buy-sell agreement or shareholders' agreement should address those issues. They can establish an up-front value for your shares of the business as well as an automatic market for those shares.

If You Want Your Business to Continue Operating

If you want your business to continue as a going concern after you die and it is a sole proprietorship or a family-owned business, then as part of your estate planning you must identify your successor. Your successor could be a family member, an employee, or someone else.

A written plan helps ensure a smooth transition from yourself to your successor. The plan should address the future management and ownership of your business, the roles and responsibilities of the future owner, and other relevant financial and legal business issues. Hire an estate planning attorney with expertise in business matters to help you develop an ironclad succession plan.

Here are some of the issues to consider prior to preparing your plan:

- Who will have primary decision-making responsibility for the business?
- How will any profits your business earns be divided up? For example, if you want your children to take over your business, do you want the children who will be most actively involved in running it to get the greater share of its profits, or do you want each of them to get the same share?
- Should some family members have voting stock and others have nonvoting stock?
- If your business is sold after you die, do you want your beneficiaries to have ongoing roles in the business? If so, what should these roles be?
- How should the sale of your business be structured?

If you want your business to continue after you die, and if you are relying on it to provide either short-term or long-term income to your family, it's a good idea to identify your successor while you're still actively involved in the business. That way, you can provide her with the training and on-the-job experience she needs to fill your shoes. Also, you will have an opportunity to assess whether she really has what it takes to fill your shoes and your successor can make sure that she really

H O T   T I P

You can give your business successor legal power to run your business should you become mentally or physically incapacitated and unable to make your own business decisions.

wants the job. If either of you has second thoughts about the planned succession, you can select a new successor.

If you choose one of your children as your successor and your business is a closely held corporation in which you own 100 percent of the shares, you must decide whether to leave the entire business to that child or just a majority interest. If you choose the first option, to be fair you may want to give your other children assets that are equal in value to the value of your business or structure some other financial arrangement that benefits them as much as you benefit the child who inherits your business. You face the same fairness issue if one of your children takes over your sole proprietorship or your share of a partnership.

HOT TIP

Key person insurance is a good way to provide funds for the continued operation of your business after your death and until your successor is in place.

Once you have decided what you want to have happen to your business after your death, openly discuss your wishes with your family. You want to be sure that everyone understands and is comfortable with your plans. Otherwise, you risk the possibility that family discord may surface after your death, which could jeopardize the stability of your business.

Transferring Ownership

If you want to leave your share of your family-owned partnership or corporation to your children or spouse after your death so that it can continue operating and generating income for them, you must decide how best to transfer ownership. One option, if your business is incorporated, is to give your family members shares of stock, possibly as annual *inter vivos* gifts. This approach also reduces the size of your estate for tax purposes.

Another option is to take advantage of the unlimited marital tax deduction by leaving your business or your share of the business to your spouse. Although this approach provides your estate with tax benefits, it can create future estate tax problems for your spouse. Your spouse faces the same potential problem if your business is a sole proprietorship. You can learn more about the unlimited marital tax deduction in Chapter 6.

Another option is to leave the family member who will own your business enough money to purchase all of its stock. One way to provide the funds for that purchase is to buy a life insurance policy and name that future owner as beneficiary.

Liquidating Your Business Assets

If there is no one in your life that you want to succeed you as owner of your business, if you don't want your business to continue after your death, or if it is unlikely that your business will be able to continue because your knowledge and/or skills are integral to its success, your best option may be to liquidate it. Liquidating a business involves selling its assets.

To prepare for a liquidation, develop an inventory of your business assets, including your accounts receivable. Describe and provide a current value for each asset. Update the inventory on a regular basis to ensure that it remains an accurate reflection of your business assets over time. Keep the inventory with your will.

You may want to include with your inventory a list of reputable business liquidators, including their names, addresses, and phone numbers, so your family will not have to develop that information themselves after your death.

Estate Taxes

As you already learned in this chapter, if you want your business to continue after you die so that it generates income for your family and if you believe that your estate will be liable for taxes, it is critical that you determine how those estate taxes will be paid. Otherwise, your family may be forced to sell your business or to sell key assets owned by your business to pay the taxes.

An estate planning attorney can help you determine how your business fits into your estate planning and what you can do to minimize your estate taxes and protect your business. Here are some tax minimization strategies you may want to consider:

- *If your business is a corporation, reduce the value of your taxable estate by giving away up to $10,000 worth of your company's stock each year to each of your children or to others ($20,000 a year if you and your spouse both make the gifts).*
- *Take advantage of the unlimited marital deduction by leaving your business to your surviving spouse.* If you use this deduction, however, you may be creating potential tax problems for your spouse depending on the value of her estate at the time of her death and the kind of estate planning she does. One way to deal with this potential problem is to place some or all of your business in a bypass trust and make your spouse the beneficiary of the trust.
- *Sell your business to your children or to someone else while you're alive.* Be aware, however, that you will have to pay taxes on the profit you realize from the sale.
- *Establish a grantor-retained annuity trust (GRAT) if your business is closely held.* This irrevocable trust provides your estate with federal tax benefits and also pays you a fixed amount of money for a specified period of time. When that time is up, the assets in the trust—company stock or other income-producing assets—transfer to the trust beneficiary.

Probate and Your Business

The probate process can inhibit efficient business decision making and damage your business in the process. Therefore, depending on how your business is structured, you may want to protect it from probate. One way to do that is to place your business in a living trust; another option is to own it as a joint tenant. Again, seek the advice of your estate planning attorney.

HOT TIP

If your business has a substantial amount of debt, placing it in a living trust may not be a good option as the trust will not protect your business against the claims of its creditors.

5

Your Children and Your Estate

Parents of minor children face special issues and concerns when planning their estates. This chapter discusses those matters and provides advice and options for addressing them. It also provides information about special issues related to leaving property to adult children.

Naming a Personal Guardian for Your Minor Child

Chapter 1 explained that if you're the parent of a minor child, depending on your state the only way you can legally designate a personal guardian for that child—the person who would raise her should both you and your spouse die—is through your will. You should also designate an alternate personal guardian who would act as your child's guardian if your first choice were unable or unwilling to carry out that responsibility should the time come.

You can name two people as coguardians for your minor child if you want. This arrangement may make sense if the coguardians are married or in a committed, unmarried relationship. However, in a society where an estimated 50 percent of all marriages fail, you may be creating potential problems down the road if the coguardians divorce or the coguardians' unmarried partnership ends.

If you have more than one young child, you can name a different guardian for each child or one guardian for all of your children. Which arrangement makes the most sense depends on your family's situation.

HOT TIP

In some states, only married couples can be named as coguardians.

On Valentine's Day, 1994, Jerry Garcia, leader of The Grateful Dead rock band, married his third wife, Carolyn Koons. On May 12, 1994, he signed his last will. A little more than a year later, on August 9, Garcia died.

Garcia was legendary at his death. His music and the man himself had attracted myriad followers over his 30-year career, including the Deadheads, the name given his most ardent fans. His fans as well as many others mourned his death. To many of us, he was a link to the counterculture revolution of the 1960s.

Although we associate Garcia with the counterculture, he wrote a very traditional will that showed great concern for his family. For example, he appointed Sunshine May Walker Kesey as guardian of his minor child, Keelin Garcia. She would be the person to raise Keelin if her mother, Manasha Matheson, did not survive him.

After your death, a court must confirm the appointment of your child's guardian, a process that is usually completed without a hitch unless someone comes forward to contest the appointment. If there are problems, a hearing will be held to determine what is in the best interest of your child.

If you die without naming a legal guardian for your minor child, it is possible that a family member or close friend may begin raising your child, acting as a *de facto* guardian (guardian in fact). The *de facto* guardian may not encounter any problems with that status unless she tries to add your child to her family's health insurance policy or enroll the child in school, needs to arrange surgery for your child, or tries to take some other action on behalf of your child that requires the consent of a parent or legal guardian. At that point, the *de facto* guardian would have to initiate a legal process to become your child's legal guardian. The court may name the *de facto* guardian legal guardian of your child, or it may decide to appoint an adult family member, close friend, or someone else. It is possible that the person who becomes your child's legal guardian may be someone you don't like or who doesn't share your values or your attitudes toward child rearing.

HOT TIP

In some states, you can use your will to stipulate whom you do *not* want to serve as your child's guardian in addition to whom you *do* want.

HOT TIP

If you have reason to expect that your child's legal guardianship may be contested, it's a good idea to leave money in your will to help pay for an attorney to fight the contest.

If You Are Divorced or Separated

If you are divorced or separated and have custody of your child, when you die, by law, your ex-spouse would ordinarily get full legal responsibility for the child. Should that parent die too, the person who would end up raising your child would probably be whomever she named in her will as your child's personal guardian, assuming your ex-spouse wrote a will.

If you would prefer that your ex-spouse not raise your child, you can say so in your will and name the person you prefer to have that responsibility. However, because your reasons for making this request are probably not flattering to your ex, it's usually not a good idea to state them in your will. If you do, your ex-spouse may sue your estate for libel. It may be better to provide your executor with a written statement of your reasons for asking that your ex-spouse not raise the child. If you have any records or other documents that support your request, attach copies of them to the statement. Also, if you have the resources, leave money in your will for your executor or one of your beneficiaries to pursue a contest of guardianship should your ex-spouse begin raising your child despite your wishes. If you do, be sure to talk with your executor or beneficiary to explain why you want the contest.

Despite what your will says, the truth is that a judge would probably award child custody to your ex-spouse unless she does not want that responsibility or unless the court decides that she is an unfit parent. Ongoing problems with drugs or alcohol, a criminal record, a history of serious mental illness, a failure to be actively involved in your child's life for a long time, among other things, could induce a judge to make that determination.

H O T   T I P

If you want to do what you can to ensure that your ex-spouse does not gain custody of your minor child, talk with an attorney who specializes in family law. Remember, though, it's a long shot.

Qualities to Look For When Choosing a Personal Guardian

It goes without saying that the person you choose as personal guardian for your child should be someone of good character whom you trust to do a responsible and caring job of raising your child. That person should also share your basic values and be willing to respect any special wishes you may have regarding how you want your child brought up. For example, you may want your child to be raised in a specific religion, or perhaps you do not want your child to receive any religious education at all. Obviously, your child's personal guardian should not have a drug or alcohol problem or a history of emotional problems. Most important, however, that person should have the time and the interest in taking on the role of guardian.

Many grandparents end up raising their grandchildren because the children's parents did not write a will or did not designate a personal guardian for their kids in their wills. However, compared to someone younger, a grandparent is more apt to become seriously ill or to die while a child is still a minor. Furthermore, a grandparent may not have the energy and stamina necessary to raise a young and active child and may also have a tougher time than a younger adult coping with some of the issues that many of today's parents have to deal with as their children grow up. Those might include issues related to drugs, sexuality, the Internet, violence, and so on.

If your child is old enough to have opinions regarding whom she would like as her guardian, ask her unless you think that having the conversation would be emotionally upsetting for your child. Listen carefully if your child raises serious objections to a potential guardian.

Leaving Property to a Minor Child

Jerry Garcia was quite specific in his will about what his children would receive from his estate after he died. For example, he gave his youngest child, Keelin Garcia, a one-half interest in a house he owned along with a share of his estate.

On the other hand, Clark Gable, a famous movie star best remembered as Rhett Butler in the movie *Gone with the Wind,* never included his child in his will. While Gable was filming his final movie, *The Misfits,* with Marilyn Monroe, his wife announced she was pregnant. In the will in effect at the time, Gable had declared that he had no children, although stories contradicted this statement. Five months later, Gable died suddenly.

By all accounts, Gable was looking forward to the birth of his child, telling everyone he hoped it would be a son. In fact, he said that when his son was born, he planned to retire and spend the rest of his life taking care of the child. Unfortunately, Gable died before he ever saw his son, John Clark Gable, and before he had a chance to amend his will to provide for his child.

Your options for transferring assets to a minor child include the following:

- Leave money and other property to your spouse or to another adult with the express understanding that they will be used for your child's benefit.
- Use your will to leave money and other property to your minor child, as Jerry Garcia did.
- Name your child as beneficiary of your insurance policy, employee benefits plan, or IRA.
- Leave money and other property to your minor child through the Uniform Gifts to Minors Acts (UGMA) or the Uniform Transfers to Minors Act (UTMA), laws discussed later in this chapter.
- Set up a trust for your child.

You may decide to use just one of these options or a combination of them to transfer your assets to your child. Each option is discussed in a subsequent section of this chapter. Their advantages and disadvantages are outlined in Figure 5.1.

H O T   T I P

A simple option for leaving relatively small amounts of money to a minor child is to make the child the beneficiary of a payable-on-death account. Although this option is not covered in this chapter, you can learn about it by reading Chapter 4.

The law in every state assumes that children younger than 18 or 21, depending on the state, do not have the knowledge or the maturity necessary to make wise decisions about substantial amounts of money and other assets and therefore need an adult to manage those assets for them. Also, children do not have the legal right to enter into contracts or to buy and sell real estate, stocks, bonds, and other property, actions that may be necessary depending on the types of assets you leave them. Therefore, although the dollar maximum varies by state, if you use your will to leave your child more than $2,500 to $5,000 worth of assets, typically you need to name a property guardian for your child in your will. This person will manage the assets on your child's behalf if you die while the child is still a minor.

FIGURE 5.1

Advantages and Disadvantages of Options for Transferring Property to a Minor Child

Option	Advantages	Disadvantages
1. Leave money and other property in your will to your spouse or another for the benefit of your child	• No need for a property guardian • Involves no extra expense or paperwork	• No guarantee that your child will actually benefit from the money and other property • Assumes that spouse or other is a good financial manager
2. Leave money and other property to your minor child in your will	• Involves no extra expense or paperwork	• Goes through probate • Depending on value of what you leave your child, you must appoint a property guardian • Your child will receive money and other property at age 18 or 21, depending on your state
3. Name your child as beneficiary of your life insurance policy, employee benefits plan, IRA	• Avoids probate • Involves no extra expense or paperwork	• Depending on value of death benefits, you must appoint a property guardian • Your child will have full control of benefits at age 18 or 21, depending on your state
4. Use the UGMA or UTMA	• Custodial accounts are easy to use and relatively inexpensive to set up • Account custodian, not property guardian, manages assets	• Irrevocable • In most states, your child will take control of money and other assets at age 18 or 21, depending on your state • You must set up a separate account for each child
5. Set up a trust for your child	• Offers maximum flexibility and control over disbursement of trust income and when child takes control of trust assets • Trustee manages assets in trust	• Relatively expensive to set up • Depending on type of trust, can be time-consuming to set up

Leaving Money and Other Property to Another Adult for Your Minor Child's Benefit

An extremely simple option for leaving property to a minor child is to leave it to your spouse or to another adult in your will, stipulating that the property must be used for your child's benefit. You can even spell out the specific things you want the assets to be used for—to help fund your child's college education, for example.

This option has a few minor advantages. First, you don't have to name a property guardian for your child because you are leaving the assets you want him to benefit from to your spouse or another adult, not directly to your child. Second, this option does not involve any additional expense or extra legal paperwork. Furthermore, the adult to whom you leave the assets is not legally obligated to maintain any records or report to the court regarding the assets.

Despite the advantages of this option, it presents some important potential disadvantages, especially if the value of the property you've earmarked for your minor child is substantial. For one thing, the option gives you absolutely no control over how the assets you want to go to your child will be managed or even whether they will be used for your child's benefit despite what you state in your will. The option also assumes that the adult you leave the property to will never be tempted to use the assets for her own benefit. Yet another drawback to this option is that if the adult you leave the assets to dies without a will while your child is still a minor, you have no guarantee that your child will end up with the assets you intended for him.

Leaving Money and Other Property to Your Minor Child through Your Will

Including your minor child in your will offers some of the same advantages as the previous option—namely, no extra paperwork or expense. However, this option has some potentially significant drawbacks. First, if the value of the property you leave your child exceeds the dollar maximum your state says a young child can legally own without adult supervision, you must use your will to designate a property guardian to manage those assets on behalf of your child. Some states require that property guardians put up a bond, and all states require that they make periodic reports to the court. To comply with this requirement, the property guardian may need to hire an attorney or a CPA, the cost of which will come out of the property you leave your child.

Another drawback to using your will to leave assets to a minor child is that your state will require the property guardian to take a very conservative approach to the management of those assets. Therefore, the guardian may not be able to maximize their value. On the plus side, however, that requirement prevents the property guardian from jeopardizing your child's assets by putting them in high-risk investments. You will learn more about property guardians in the next section of this chapter.

Another drawback of this option is that your child will get full control of the assets you leave him in your will when he becomes a legal adult. Yet your child may not be mature enough or financially savvy enough to manage them responsibly, especially if their value is substantial or the assets are relatively complex.

HOT TIP

If you don't use your will to transfer property to a minor child, it's still a good idea to designate a property guardian for your child just in case he inherits a substantial amount of property from someone else and needs an adult to manage it.

Naming Your Child as Beneficiary of Your Life Insurance Policy, Employee Benefits Plan, or IRA

Another way to provide financially for your child in the event of your death is to make him the beneficiary of your insurance policy, employee benefits plan, or IRA. At your death, the proceeds from these assets—the death benefits—will automatically pass directly to your child, avoiding probate and the claims of creditors.

Depending on the value of the benefits, you must appoint an adult to manage them for your child until he becomes a legal adult; the benefits will not be released otherwise. If you arrange to have the benefits paid directly to your child, the adult you appoint to manage the benefits will be a property guardian. If the benefits are placed in a trust, the adult will be a trustee; and if the benefits are deposited in a custodial account under the Uniform Gifts to Minors Act or the Uniform Transfers to Minors Act, the adult in charge of those assets will be an account custodian.

Using the UGMA or UTMA

The Uniform Gifts to Minors Act (UGMA) was enacted in 1956 and applied only to *inter vivos* gifts of money and securities to minor children. In 1966, the act was amended to include insurance policies and annuities. In 1983, the Uniform Transfers to Minors Act (UTMA) was adopted. It covers real and tangible property as well as all of the types of property covered by the 1956 and 1966 versions of the UGMA. Every state has adopted a version of the UGMA or the UTMA.

Leaving assets to a minor child using the UGMA or the UTMA is simple and inexpensive. All you have to do is open a custodial account at a bank or brokerage house in the name of the person you designate as account custodian and then transfer into the account any assets you want to pass on to your child.

H O T   T I P

A UGMA or UTMA custodial account is irrevocable, which means that you cannot remove from the account anything you place in it. It is not yours anymore. Therefore, don't put in the account anything you may need later.

Low cost and ease of setup are not the only advantages of custodial accounts. Another benefit is that account custodians don't deal with the state oversight and control that property guardians have to contend with. Therefore, they can do more to maximize the value of the assets in a custodial account and increase the income they may generate.

UGMA and UTMA accounts come with some potential disadvantages too. One disadvantage is that in most states your child gets full control of the assets in the account as soon as he becomes a legal adult, regardless of whether he is emotionally and financially prepared to manage them. In some states you can extend a custodianship until your child turns 25.

A second minor drawback is that you cannot set up one custodial account for multiple children. To leave assets to more than one child, you must set up an account for each. Also, any income or gain earned by the assets in a custodial account must be reported to the IRS in your child's name as your child is the account's legal owner. If your child is younger than 14, he will be taxed at the *kiddie* tax rate. However, when your child turns 14, the tax rate will be higher.

A final disadvantage to using the UGMA or UTMA is that the assets you place in a custodial account are treated as *inter vivos* gifts. Therefore, if the total of the assets transferred into an account in a given year exceeds your annual $10,000 per person gift limit, you must file a federal gift tax return, and the excess will decrease your total federal estate tax exemption.

Account Custodians

You can name yourself custodian of your child's UGMA or UTMA account, or you can appoint someone else, like your child's other parent, another relative, or a friend. Don't forget to designate a successor custodian as well.

Account custodians are entitled to receive a fee for their services, although a relative or close friend is apt to waive the fee.

Account custodians are not subject to the state scrutiny and control that property guardians have to deal with. They are free to manage the account assets as they see fit and disburse income from an account as needed, and they have no reporting requirements to comply with.

H O T   T I P

You can appoint a financial institution or a securities broker as account custodian. Given the fees charged by a professional account custodian, however, it's usually not cost-effective to hire one unless there are a lot of assets to manage or the assets are particularly valuable and/or complex.

Setting Up a Trust for Your Minor Child

A trust is an excellent estate planning tool for transferring a substantial amount of property to a minor child. Flexibility and control over the terms of the transfer are the primary benefits of a trust. The control is a particular advantage if you are leaving your child a considerable amount of money or if the assets you are transferring to him are particularly complex. Another important benefit of a trust is that you can give the trustee considerable independence and control over the management of the assets in the trust and the dispersal of any income they generate.

Frequently, when parents set up a trust for a minor child, one parent names the other as trustee. With this arrangement, a minor child's property guardian is often the logical choice for alternate trustee because both jobs require someone who is comfortable dealing with money and investments. Another option is to name the property guardian as primary trustee and someone else as alternate.

Leaving Property to Adopted Children

No matter what their ages, your adopted children have the same inheritance rights as your biological children in most states. But if you want to be absolutely certain that they do, you have two options when you write your will. You can specifically designate each of the children you are leaving your property to or you can state that you are leaving your property to "all of my children" and then define exactly what you mean by that phrase, being sure to include your adopted children in the definition.

You have many decisions to make when you have a minor child to provide for through your estate planning. A brief review of some of the key questions to consider are listed in Figure 5.2.

If You Have Children from a Prior Marriage

If you are married, you probably want to leave all of your estate to your surviving spouse. However, if you do that through your will and you have children from a previous marriage, you have no guarantee that your spouse will plan her estate so that at least some of those assets will go to your children, especially if your spouse also has children from

---

FIGURE 5.2

Questions to Answer When Thinking about Your Estate and Your Minor Child

- Who do I want to name as my child's legal or personal guardian?

- Who do I want as my child's property guardian?

- What property do I want to pass on to my child and at what age do I want him to have access to those assets?

- What estate planning tool (or tools) should I use to convey the assets to my minor child?

- If I use the UGMA or UTMA, who should be the account custodian?

- If I set up a trust for my child, who do I want as trustee? What investment and dispersal policy do I want the trustee to adopt?

- When do I want my child to take full control of the trust property?

- Do I want my minor child to receive income from the trust? If so, for what purposes and how much?

---

a former marriage. If your spouse and children do not get along, you may have real cause for concern.

There are several ways to deal with this potential problem. They include these options:

- *You and your spouse can coordinate the provisions of your wills to provide for one another and for any children either of you has from a previous marriage.* Because either of you can change or revoke your wills at any time, however, you run the risk that your spouse's will could be changed, leaving nothing to your children.

- *You can purchase a life insurance policy, name your children as policy beneficiaries, and set up an irrevocable life insurance trust.* To make this option work, your beneficiaries, not you, must own the policy. In other words, the policy must be in their names, not yours. Since they are children, you will have to give them enough money each year to pay the insurance premiums.

- *You can use a trust.* Your attorney can help you set up a trust that would provide for your surviving spouse and then transfer the trust assets to your children after your spouse dies.

- *You can negotiate a legally binding prenuptial agreement before you get married or a postnuptial agreement after you are married.* The agreement can spell out exactly how each of you will divide up your estates after your deaths, including what you will leave to your children.

Stepchildren and Your Will

Your state inheritance laws will not treat your stepchildren as your legal heirs, which means that they do not have an automatic legal right to inherit from you. Therefore, if you want to ensure they will receive part of your estate when you die, you must make them explicit beneficiaries of your estate planning.

Leaving Property to Out-of-Wedlock Children

In most states, if you're a female and your will says that you are leaving property to "all of my children," that term includes any children you may have had outside of marriage. On the other hand, if you're a male, that definition usually includes only the children born to you and your wife as well as to any children who have proved that you are their biological father. Regardless of your sex and your state of residence, however, you can explicitly include or exclude your out-of-wedlock children when you write your will. If you have any out-of-wedlock children, it is advisable to consult with an attorney about the inheritance laws of your state.

Disinheriting a Child

Nearly all states have laws regarding *pretermitted* children, or children left out of a will. These laws say that a child who is not included in his parent's will is legally entitled to an intestate share of that parent's estate unless the will makes clear that the parent intended not to include the child. The laws vary in regard to the circumstances under which these laws apply; and how much a pretermitted child is legally entitled to inherit varies from state to state. For example, some laws apply only to children born or adopted after a will is executed, while others apply to all children regardless of when they are born.

If you want to disinherit one of your children, talk with an estate planning attorney. She can explain what your state's law says about disinheritance and help you write your will so that your wishes will be carried out. You should also explain your reasons for the disinheritance to the executor of your estate, and, depending on the circumstances, you may also want to talk with the child you are disinheriting so that your action does not come as a painful surprise after your death.

HOT TIP

If you use the general phrase "to all of my children" when you leave property to your children in your will, any children born after you have written your will usually inherit the same share of your estate as your other children.

Simply not mentioning one of your children in your will is no guarantee that the child will actually be disinherited. Also, you risk opening the door to a will contest after you die. For example, the child you left out of your will could argue that it was an oversight and that you didn't really intend to disinherit him. If your will was contested, a court would probably award the child some portion of your estate, depending on the laws of your state regarding pretermitted children. How much would depend on such factors as whether your spouse is still living and how many other children you have.

HOT TIP

An attorney will probably charge you extra to draw up a will that disinherits your child as she will have to take extra steps to make sure that the disinheritance stands up in court.

Leaving Property to Adult Children

You can transfer property to your adult children using any of the estate planning tools you might use to transfer property to any other adult beneficiary. Depending on your family situation, however, you may want to address special issues related to your adult children in your estate planning. For example, if some of your children are much better off financially than others, or if some of them have children and others don't, you may want to leave some of your children more than others. Also, if one of your children is a poor money manager and you plan on leaving him a substantial amount of assets, you may want to be sure that he does not squander the inheritance. One way to do that is to set up a spendthrift trust. Typically, this trust is set up to last until the beneficiary turns 50. The thinking is that by that age, even a spendthrift will have matured!

If you have an adult child who is mentally or physically handicapped and unable to earn a living or manage his own finances, you can set up a trust to provide for that child throughout his life.

6

Probate, Taxes, and Your Estate

Most people have two key estate planning goals. One goal is to ensure that as much of their estate as possible goes to their beneficiaries rather than having their estate depleted by probate, taxes, and other expenses. The other goal is to ensure that their estate transfers to their beneficiaries as quickly as possible.

Up-front planning helps you achieve both goals. If probate is a concern to you, your planning should focus on reducing the assets in your estate that will go through probate. If your estate is small enough, your planning should ensure that the estate qualifies for the quicker and cheaper alternative to the traditional probate process that may be available in your state. And if estate taxes are an issue for you, your planning should involve minimizing the size of your taxable estate.

This chapter focuses most of its attention on the probate process for two key reasons. First, the costs and delays associated with probate are probably of concern to you regardless of how much your estate is worth. Second, if you are like most people, the value of your estate is too low for you to be concerned about estate taxes, especially given the recent changes in the law.

The chapter also discusses alternatives to the traditional, formal probate process that are available to small estates in many states. It also offers a general overview of estate taxes as well as some suggestions for how to reduce them.

What Is Probate?

Probate is a legal process that will prove the validity of your will after you die so that the assets described in it can be distributed to your beneficiaries. More specifically, however, probate encompasses all of the activities over which the probate court has jurisdiction. Among other things, this includes:

- Formally appointing your executor
- Determining the validity of your will
- Identifying and valuing all of the assets in your estate
- Paying your estate's debts and taxes as well as all probate-related fees
- Distributing the assets in your probate estate to your beneficiaries

Assuming the probate court in your county of residence approves the executor named in your will, she will shepherd your estate through the probate process. Although it rarely happens, if the state doesn't approve your choice for executor, it will appoint an administrator for your estate who will perform all of the duties your executor would have carried out. The court may deny approval if it doesn't feel that your choice is capable of carrying out the responsibilities of the job or if one or more of your heirs formally objects to your choice of executor and the court upholds their objection.

You learned in Chapter 1 that only those assets in your estate that pass under your will go through probate. These assets include:

- All assets you own in your own name
- Your share of any assets you own as a tenant in common
- One-half of your community property, if you own property in a community property state
- Life insurance death benefits when your estate is the beneficiary
- Property placed in a testamentary trust

See Figure 6.1 for a list of the assets that do not go through probate.

Potential Drawbacks of Probate

When people hear the word *probate,* a lot of negatives tend to come to mind. Most people think of the probate process as expensive, excessively time-consuming for an executor, and needlessly slow in

---

FIGURE 6.1
Assets That Are Not Probated

Not all of the assets in your estate go through probate. Therefore, one strategy for reducing the time and expense of probate is to maximize the assets you own that don't have to be probated. Assets that do not go through probate include these:

- Jointly owned property—property that you own as a joint tenant with right of survivorship or as a tenant by the entirety

- *Inter vivos* gifts

- Assets placed in trust accounts

- Death benefits from IRAs, life insurance policies, and employee benefits plans as long as your estate is not the beneficiary

- Property placed in a living trust

- Some business property controlled by contracts

- Depending on your state, community property that goes to a spouse

---

transferring property to the beneficiaries of a will. With the right planning, however, you can eliminate most of the negatives or at least minimize their impact. For example, although the duration of the probate process tends to vary from six months to one year, the duration can be longer or shorter depending on such factors as these:

- The number, value, and complexity of the assets in your probate estate
- The number of beneficiaries in your will
- Whether anyone contests the validity of your will or challenges one of its provisions
- The number of creditor claims against your estate
- The probate laws of your state
- The efficiency of the court that oversees your estate's probate process
- Whether your estate must file an estate tax return
    If it does, it could take as long as two to three years before everything is settled with the IRS.
- Whether your will can be located immediately after your death

- If the witnesses to the signing of your will can't be found or, if they are not alive at the time of your death, whether there is a self-proving affidavit
- How long it takes to locate and value the assets in your estate

Another drawback for many people is probate's public nature. Anyone who wants to can read a copy of someone's will once it has been filed with the court and can obtain a copy of the will.

The Costs of Probate

Studies show that the expenses of the formal probate process can eat up at least 10 percent of your estate—these may include court costs, appraisal costs, fees paid to your executor, and attorney fees—but there are ways to minimize your estate's probate costs after you die. For example, by carefully planning your estate and by writing a legally valid and clearly worded will, you decrease the potential that problems will crop up during the probate process that will cost your estate money to resolve. Also, another way to keep your probate costs down is to select a competent executor who can do some of the work that an attorney would otherwise do. In fact, if your estate is relatively small and simple and if the probate process goes off without a hitch, your executor may not need an attorney's help at all because the executor's job will be mainly pulling together information and filling out forms. Nonetheless, nearly every executor uses an attorney for at least some aspect of the probate process. In fact, not using one can be penny-wise and pound-foolish because an attorney may be able to save an executor time and money.

HOT TIP

A problem-free estate with no tax liability usually pays about $1,000 in probate-related attorney fees and court costs. The cost could be higher or lower, however, depending on where your estate is probated. The costs of probate vary by state.

Another strategy for reducing the costs of probate is to pass as much of it as possible over or outside your will rather than under it. This strategy can be especially cost-effective if your state uses the value of an estate to determine the estate's probate fees.

Court Costs

In most states, the probate-related court costs that an estate must pay are relatively insignificant, maybe just a few hundred dollars at the most. Those costs may include filing fees, registration fees, publication fees, and fees based on the value of your probate estate.

Appraisal Costs

Appraisal costs during probate pay for the process of valuing the property in your probate estate. Usually, an appraiser is used to place a value on assets other than cash, publicly traded securities, and similar assets—real estate, fine antiques, expensive jewelry, or rare stamps, for example. If your estate is modest, appraisal costs may range from a few hundred dollars to a few thousand, depending on the amount and types of assets. However, those costs can be a lot more if there are many assets to appraise or if some of your assets are unusual and must be appraised by a specialist.

Fiduciary Fees

Fiduciary fees are the fees to which your executor is entitled; court-appointed administrators are also entitled to those fees. States limit how much an executor can receive in fees, and the fees must be approved by the probate court before they can be paid. As Chapter 1 mentioned, family members and close friends who serve as executors often waive the right to receive any fees for their services to your estate.

Fiduciary fees are either calculated as a percentage of the net value of your estate or are determined on the basis of "reasonableness," as defined by your state. If they are based on an estate's net value, that value is the total appraised value of all the property in your estate less the total amount of debt that is secured by that property.

Attorney Fees

As this chapter has already indicated, most executors use an attorney to help them with the probate process. Attorneys typically charge for their services on an hourly basis, and there is a wide range in their hourly rates—anywhere from about $50 an hour to more than $200 an hour. In part, an attorney's rate depends on whether your estate is being probated in an urban or rural area and on the East or West Coast rather than in between. The rate is also determined by the size of the law firm your estate's attorney works for—lawyers with large, high-profile firms tend to charge more than attorneys who work for smaller firms—as well as on the attorney's level of experience. Seasoned attorneys tend to charge more per hour than relative newcomers to the legal profession.

Potential Benefits of Probate

For all the negatives associated with the probate process, there are also benefits. First, the process helps ensure that only those individuals or organizations with true claims to your estate will get your property after you die. Second, it protects your estate by limiting the amount of time that creditors with claims against it can try to get paid by your estate. The period of time is usually somewhere between four and six months. Creditors that don't present their claims before the end of this period cannot take collection action against your estate.

HOT TIP

If an estate attorney tells you that she will charge for her probate-related services by taking a percentage of your estate's value, look for another attorney. Reputable attorneys do not charge this way; they charge by the hour for time worked.

How the Formal Probate Process Works

Even though the formal probate process varies from state to state, the following is a helpful overview of the typical steps in that process.

Step 1. After you die, the person you name in your will as your executor files paperwork with the probate court in your area.

Step 2. Usually, the court formally appoints that person as executor. The court also makes sure that your will is legally valid. If you did not write a will, it appoints an administrator to do what an executor would do on behalf of your estate.

Step 3. Your executor presents the court with a list of your assets and debts.

Step 4. Your executor formally notifies your legal heirs as well as your creditors of your death. Your heirs and creditors will have a set amount of time—usually several months—to file claims against your estate. It is during this period that a disgruntled heir might contest the validity of your will. Figure 6.2 provides a list of grounds for contesting a will. If no claims are filed against your estate and no one contests the validity

---

 FIGURE 6.2
Grounds for Contesting a Will

When there is a contest or challenge to your will, the court will consider it only when the individual or business making the contest or challenge has legal grounds for its action. Those grounds are:

- Improper execution

- Lack of testamentary capacity (you were mentally incompetent when you prepared your will or were under the influence of drugs or alcohol)

- Undue influence

- Fraud

- Forgery

of your will, the court will formally approve your will and admit it to probate.

Step 5. Your executor prepares and files a final list of the assets in your probate estate, files tax returns if necessary, and gets ready to transfer those assets to your beneficiaries according to the instructions in your will.

Step 6. Your estate pays all legitimate creditor claims, including the claims of taxing authorities that filed their claims within the allotted period of time. If your executor contests the validity or amount of a claim, this step may take considerable time to complete. None of your beneficiaries will receive the assets you have left them until this process is finished.

Step 7. Your executor completes all final paperwork, prepares a final report for the court, and petitions the court to close your estate. This won't happen until all required fees and expenses have been paid and all issues related to your estate have been resolved. Your legal heirs can contest the executor's final accounting; if they do, the court holds a hearing.

Step 8. The probate judge formally closes your estate and releases your executor from any further duties.

The Family Allowance

Most states allow a surviving spouse and any dependent children she and the deceased had together during their marriage to receive a family allowance while the deceased's estate is being probated The allowance, which is paid by the estate, helps ensure that a family does not suffer financially during the process.

The amount of a family allowance varies from state to state. Some states pay a set amount regardless of family size or other factors. Others consider a number of factors when deciding on the amount of a family allowance. Typically, those factors include the overall financial status of the surviving spouse and the number of dependent children she must raise on her own now that her husband is dead.

Some states also protect a surviving spouse and minor children from losing their homestead to creditors. These states also prohibit the heirs or beneficiaries of the deceased spouse from forcing the surviving spouse to move out of the homestead, even if it has been left to the deceased's heirs or beneficiaries in full or in part.

Alternatives to the Formal Probate Process

In most states, eligible estates can use an alternative to the formal probate process. Eligible estates have the following characteristics:

- They are worth a relatively small amount of money.
- They do not include any complex assets.
- There are few beneficiaries in the will.
- They have few creditors.
- They are not liable for estate or inheritance taxes.

Because the court's involvement is minimal in the alternative probate process, the process is faster and less expensive than the formal probate process. Although their specifics vary from state to state, the alternatives to that process tend to be one of two types: *summary administration* or *collection by affidavit*. The highlights of each process are described below.

Summary Administration

Eligible estates. Any estate that has an executor, is valued at less than a state-set maximum—usually no more than $50,000—and that meets other state criteria is eligible.

How it works. The executor immediately transfers assets in the will to the appropriate beneficiaries and files a formal accounting with the court. Intermediate steps, such as the notification of creditors, the creditor waiting period, and the formal inventory and appraisal of probate assets, are eliminated.

Restrictions. The consent of all beneficiaries to a will may have to be obtained for summary administration to be used.

Collection by Affidavit

Eligible estates. Any estate whose net value is less than an amount set by the state is eligible.

How it works. Everyone who thinks he is entitled to certain personal property of the deceased completes an affidavit stating so, and the holder of the property transfers it to the person who completed the affidavit.

Restrictions. Some states allow only spouses and children to collect by affidavit; others permit only certain types of property to be collected by affidavit; and still other states mandate a minimal amount of court involvement.

Dealing with Probate

When people are faced with the probate process, they tend to have one of three goals: (1) avoid probate entirely; (2) minimize the number of assets in their estate that must go through probate; or (3) try to qualify for the more informal probate process if it is available to them. To accomplish any of those three goals, you should consider doing the following:

- Own as many assets as possible as a joint tenant with right of survivorship.
- Own assets with your spouse as a tenant by the entirety.
- Make someone the beneficiary of your life insurance policy, employee benefits plan, or IRA.
- Make *inter vivos* gifts.
- Set up informal trust accounts.
- Establish a living trust.

It is important that you discuss your estate vis-à-vis the probate process with your attorney. To prepare for that discussion, you may want to return to Chapters 1 and 4, which discuss in detail the probate avoidance and minimization options just outlined.

HOT TIP

Avoiding probate may be an admirable goal, but in truth it's hard to do. Even with the best estate planning, it's easy to overlook an asset. That oversight could mean that your estate would go through probate after all, despite your planning.

Taxes and Your Estate

When you die, your estate may have to pay taxes. The more taxes it must pay, the less will be left to be distributed to your beneficiaries. Therefore, for those with substantial estates, tax minimization is an important part of estate planning. Depending on your state, taxes may be an issue even if your estate is not worth a lot.

Following are some of the taxes your estate may have to pay.

Estate income tax. Your estate must pay this tax if the income it earns in any tax year exceeds the standard exemptions an estate receives.

Personal income tax. This is the tax due on your income in the year of your death.

Federal estate tax. Your estate must pay this tax only if its value exceeds a certain dollar amount. The amount is based on the current market value of all the assets in your estate, not just those that go through probate. The amount is known as the *unified tax credit*. In 2001, the amount of this tax credit is $675,000. Therefore if your estate is worth $700,000 at the time of your death and you were to die in 2001, $25,000 of your estate would be subject to federal estate taxes. The federal estate tax ranges between 37 percent and 55 percent.

A new law passed in 2001, authorizing gradual increases in the size of the unified tax credit and an end to the federal estate tax, but for just one year. After that year ends, the federal estate tax will be reinstated, but there are questions regarding the size of the unified tax credit at that point. Therefore, check with an estate planning attorney for the most up-to-date information, especially because at this writing there is talk that the new estate tax law may be repealed or changed. The increases stop in 2009. Here are the amounts of the unified tax credit for the years 2002–2009:

2002	$1,000,000	2007	$2,000,000
2003	$1,000,000	2008	$2,000,000
2004	$1,500,000	2009	$3,500,000
2005	$1,500,000	2010	No federal estate tax
2006	$2,000,000	2011	Either $1,000,000 or $3,500,000

State estate tax. A few states have their own estate taxes, although those states are growing fewer and fewer in number. Although these states may impose their tax on estates valued at less than the federal

---

H O T   T I P

If in any year, you make an *inter vivos* gift to someone that is worth more than $10,000, the excess will be deducted from the total amount of your unified tax credit.

---

estate tax threshold, potentially affecting more modest estates, the good news is that their tax rates are considerably lower than the federal government's.

The inheritance tax. Some states tax the inheritance a beneficiary may receive. The tax is levied against the value of the inheritance, but a trend is growing among the states to eliminate this tax; and at the time this book was written, less than one-fourth of the states still had this tax.

Appendix B includes examples of some of the IRS forms that your executor may have to file for your estate after your death.

The Unlimited Marital Tax Deduction

The unlimited marital tax deduction gives married people a break on their federal estate taxes. It allows you to leave all of your estate to your spouse without incurring any estate tax liability regardless of your estate's value.

H O T   T I P

The unlimited marital deduction is not available to spouses who are not citizens of this country except through a qualified domestic trust.

Although this deduction provides an undeniable immediate benefit to your surviving spouse, without the right estate planning it can create future tax problems for your spouse's estate. This is because use of the unlimited tax deduction only postpones payment of your estate taxes as they will have to be paid by the estate of your surviving spouse when she dies. Furthermore, if your surviving spouse owns assets in her own name, and if the assets you leave your spouse appreciate after your death, your spouse's estate could face a substantial tax liability.

If you feel that using the unlimited marital deduction may create future tax problems for your spouse, talk with an estate planning attorney. The attorney may recommend that you set up a trust to get around the problem.

Strategies to Reduce Your Estate Taxes

If it appears that your estate will owe taxes, there are ways to reduce that liability or even wipe it out. Determine your best strategy in consultation with an estate planning attorney. Figure 6.3 presents six tax-reduction options.

FIGURE 6.3
Six Ways to Reduce Your Estate Taxes

1. Use the unlimited marital tax deduction.

2. Make *inter vivos* gifts. You can give up to $10,000 each year to as many people as you want.

3. Make *inter vivos* gifts to bona fide charities. Your state may place limits on the amount you can give.

4. Place property in an irrevocable trust.

5. Have your spouse, another adult, or an irrevocable trust purchase a life insurance policy to pay your estate taxes and make someone else the owner of that policy. That "someone else" can be your spouse, your child, another adult, or an irrevocable trust. Whoever owns the policy must pay the policy premiums. If you make the payments, you will be considered the policy owner and will not realize any tax benefits. If the life insurance policy is purchased at least three years before your death, the proceeds from the policy will not be considered part of your taxable estate.

6. Spend the assets in your estate before you die.

If Your Estate Must Pay Taxes

The taxes your estate may owe must be paid before your beneficiaries can receive what you have left them. If you made special provisions in your will for paying your taxes, your executor will follow them. Otherwise, your executor will use the money in your residuary estate to pay your taxes.

If your residuary estate does not have enough money to pay all of the taxes your estate owes, payment of those taxes will be apportioned among all of the assets in your estate, starting with general bequests and then moving to specific bequests. Personal property will be tapped before real property. As a result, your beneficiaries may end up with less than what you had intended them to receive. Unless all estate-related taxes are paid to the IRS, the agency will use any of the tools available to it to collect its money, including seizing assets and levying bank accounts.

7

Sample Wills

This chapter features several sample wills. Together with the celebrity wills in Appendix A and the commentary on those celebrity wills that runs throughout this book, they illustrate the general format and typical wording of various types of wills as well as the kinds of provisions a will can include.

This chapter also provides a number of different clauses you can use to address specific situations. In addition, it includes a sample self-proving affidavit.

Explanations for and Limitations of Sample Wills

You can say pretty much whatever you want in your will and however you want to say it because for the most part there are no laws that govern what you state in a will. However, certain terms and phrases have become matters of convention. Also, when you write your will, it is best to use precise, unambiguous words to express your wishes. Otherwise, after you die there may be questions about what you meant by a particular sentence or clause. Worst-case scenario: There may be such a difference of opinion among your heirs regarding your wishes that a judge would have to decide what you meant.

The wills in this chapter as well as in Appendix A illustrate how wills are typically worded. They also illustrate the fact that there is no set length for a will. A well-written will that accomplishes your goals can be long or short. It depends, among other things, on the number of assets you have to give away, whether you establish a testamentary trust, the number of beneficiaries in your will, and so on.

One note of caution regarding the sample wills in this chapter: If you find one that fits your general circumstances, don't assume that you can use it as the basis for writing your own will. Talk with an attorney so that you can be sure that you end up with a will that meets your estate planning goals and meets the specific requirements of your state for a legally valid will. Also, as you have already learned in this book, another important reason for meeting with an attorney is that she can make you aware of things you should address in your will as well as help you ensure that you do not create financial and/or legal problems for your heirs because your estate planning was inadequate. The attorney can also suggest other estate planning tools in addition to a will you should use depending on your circumstances.

As you read through the sample wills here, you will notice that some of the selected clauses in the samples are followed by italicized explanations. Please note, however, that an explanation appears only the first time a clause is used; it is not repeated in subsequent wills.

Sample Will for a Single Person with Minor Children

An estimated 50 percent of all American marriages ends in divorce. Unfortunately, therefore, this type of will applies to a large and ever-increasing number of people.

Last Will and Testament
of
(your name)

Clause 1

I, *(your name)*, a resident in *(your city and state of residence)*, being of sound mind and not acting under any duress, fraud, or undue influence of any person, declare this instrument as my Last Will and Testament.

If you own property in a name different from the one you use in this will, or if you changed your name and use that new name in your will, insert the following phrase into the clause above.

1. *(your name)*, also known as *(other name/s)*

Be sure to share your other name (or names) with your attorney.

Revocation

I revoke all prior wills and codicils by me.

Even if you have no recollection of ever having written a will, include this clause in your will. It's a matter of being on the safe side, just in case your memory is poor.

Clause 3: Identification of Family

I am presently unmarried. I am the *(mother/father)* of the following children, all living at the time this will was written and executed:

_____	_____
(name of child)	*(date of birth)*
_____	_____
(name of child)	*(date of birth)*

If you were previously married, add a paragraph that states the name of your former spouse(s) and why the marriage(s) ended. I was formerly married to *(name of former spouse)*. This marriage ended by *(specify divorce, annulment, or death)*.

Clause 4: Appointment of Executor

I appoint *(name of executor)* as executor of this will. If *(he/she)* cannot or will not serve in this capacity, I appoint *(name of substitute executor)* as my substitute executor. *You can also name coexecutors.* In addition to all the powers allowable under the laws of this state, I authorize and empower my executor to *(itemize all of the additional powers and responsibilities, if any, you give to your executor)*.

I request that my executor be allowed to act without having to post any bond or other kind of security.

Typical additional powers and responsibilities you can give to your executor include

- *the freedom to retain the property in your estate without liability for its depreciation or loss;*
- *the ability to sell, lease, or exchange, by public or private means, real or personal property and to administer any proceeds as appropriate;*
- *the freedom to exercise all of the rights of a person who owns securities;*
- *the freedom to pay all legal claims against your estate, including any debts you owed at the time of your death and any estate taxes that may arise from your death, provided that such debts and taxes are paid first from your residuary estate;*
- *the right to operate, sell, encumber, maintain, or dispose of any business or part of a business that is in your estate;*
- *the right to distribute property to the guardian, custodian, or trustee for the benefit of any minor children you have;*
- *the freedom to defend or settle any claims for or against your estate; and*
- *the right to take all other actions that your executor feels are necessary and appropriate for the proper management, investment, and distribution of your estate.*

Elvis Presley made his dad, Vernon, the executor of his estate and trustee of his trusts. Sadly, the responsibility was too much for Vernon, and Elvis's estate was nearly wasted away under his stewardship. At the time of Vernon's death, the cost of running Graceland was $480,000 a year, and annual revenues generated by Elvis Presley Enterprises had begun dipping below $500,000.

Elvis's will includes provisions for a trust to be set up at his death for his daughter, Lisa Marie. It says that she should get control of the trust assets when she turned 25 and would receive the bulk of his estate on Februrary 1, 1998, when she turned 30. To make sure that her daughter would have an inheritance after Vernon died, Elvis's ex-wife, Priscilla Presley, took over Elvis Enterprises, turning it into a $100 million estate.

Clause 5: Appointment of Guardian

In the event I shall die leaving any of my children as minors and my former spouse does not survive me, I appoint as personal and property guardian of my minor children *(name of guardian)*. If *(he/she)* dies, resigns, or is otherwise unable to serve as personal and property guardian, I appoint *(name of alternate guardian)* as successor guardian.

The guardian shall serve without bond or surety and without the intervention of any court except as required by law.

You can name a different guardian for each child if that makes practical sense. You can also name different people to serve as personal and property guardians.

Jerry Garcia appointed Sunshine May Walker Kesey as the guardian of Keelin Garcia, his minor daughter, if her mother did not survive him.

Clause 6: Disposition of Property

I give all of my estate to my children to be divided among them in equal shares. If one of my children shall not survive me by 30 days, the surviving child should receive all of the aforementioned gift. If neither child survives me by 30 days, my estate is to be distributed as follows:

I give *(name of beneficiary)* my *(description of property)*, if *(he/she)* survives me by 60 days. If *(he/she)* does not survive me, I give the above-described property to *(name of alternate beneficiary)*, if *(he/she)* survives me. If neither of the above persons survives me, the above-described property should be disposed of with the residue of my estate.

Repeat the above clause if necessary.

I give the sum of $ *(dollar amount)* to *(name of beneficiary)* if *(he/she)* survives me by 60 days. If *(he/she)* does not survive me, I give the same sum of money to *(name of alternate beneficiary)* if *(he/she)* survives me. If neither of the above persons survives me, this same sum of money should be disposed of with the residue of my estate.

Repeat the above clause if necessary.

Clause 7: Residuary Estate

I give the rest of my estate, all the property I own that is not legally disposed of by this will or in some other manner, to *(name of residual beneficiary).* In the event *(he/she)* does not survive me by 60 days, I give the aforementioned gift to *(name of alternate beneficiary).*

    If any primary beneficiary of a shared residuary or specific gift made by me in this will fails to survive me by 60 days, the surviving beneficiaries of that gift shall equally divide between them the deceased beneficiary's share. If all primary beneficiaries of a shared residuary or specific gift fail to survive me by 60 days, that gift shall pass to the alternate beneficiaries named to receive that gift. If the alternate beneficiaries named in this will to receive a specific gift fail to survive me by 60 days, or no such named alternate beneficiaries exist, that gift shall become part of my residuary estate.

> You can find an example of a residuary clause in Marilyn Monroe's will. The residue of her estate after specific bequests went to May Reis, a friend, Dr. Marianne Kris, her psychotherapist, and to Lee Strasberg, Monroe's acting coach.

Clause 8: Signature

I subscribe my name to this will on the *(date)* day of *(month),* 20 *(year),* at *(city, county, and state),* and declare that I am a legal and competent adult and that I did not enter into or sign this will under duress, constraint, or undue influence.
(your legal signature)

Clause 9: Attestation

On this *(date)* day of *(month)* 20 *(year), (your name)* declared to us, the undersigned, that this document was *(his/her)* will and asked us to serve as witnesses, signing our names accordingly. At the request of *(your name)*, and in *(his/her)* presence, and in the presence of each other, all being present at the same time, we have signed our names as witnesses. We declare this to be the will of *(your name)*, and that to the best of our knowledge, *(your name)* is a competent adult and was under no undue influence, duress, or constraint at the time of this signing. Under penalty of perjury, we declare that the foregoing is true and correct.

_____
(witness's signature)

_____
(witness's address)

_____
(witness's signature)

_____
(witness's address)

_____
(witness's signature)

_____
(witness's address)

Sample Will for a Single Person with No Children

This is an example of a basic will that might be appropriate for young people just starting their careers and in the early stages of building their wealth.

Last Will and Testament
of
(your name)

Clause 1

I, *(your name)*, a resident in *(your city and state of residence)*, being of sound mind and not acting under any duress, fraud, or undue influence of any person, declare this instrument as my Last Will and Testament.

Clause 2: Revocation

I hereby revoke all prior wills and codicils by me.

Clause 3: Identification of Family

I am presently unmarried and have no living children.

I have never been formerly married.

If you've never been married, this clause is not necessary, but including it means that you will leave nothing to question.

Clause 4: Appointment of Executor

I appoint *(name of executor)* as executor of this will. If *(he/she)* cannot or will not serve in this capacity, I appoint *(name of substitute executor)* as my substitute executor. In addition to all of the powers allowable under the laws of this state, I authorize and empower my executor to *(itemize all of the additional powers and responsibilities you give your executor).*

I request that my executor be allowed to act without having to post any bond or other kind of security.

Clause 5: Disposition of Property

I give *(name of beneficiary)* my *(description of property)* if *(he/she)* survives me by 30 days. If *(he/she)* does not survive me by 30 days, I give the above-described property to *(name of alternate beneficiary)* if *(he/she)* survives me by 30 days. If neither of the above persons survives me by 30 days, the above-described property should be disposed of with the residue of my estate.

Repeat the above clause if necessary.

Clause 6: Residuary Estate

I give the rest of my estate, all the property I own that is not legally disposed of by this will or in some other manner, to *(name of residual beneficiary)*. In the event *(he/she)* does not survive me by 30 days, I give my residuary estate to *(name of charity)* at *(address of charity)* for the general support of its activities.

Clause 7: Signature

I subscribe my name to this will on the *(date)* day of *(month)*, 20 *(year)* at *(city, county, and state)*, and declare that I am a legal and competent adult and that I did not enter into or sign this will under duress, constraint, or undue influence.

(your legal signature)

Clause 8: Attestation

On this *(date)* day of *(month)*, 20 *(year)*, *(your name)* declared to us, the undersigned, that this document was *(his/her)* will and asked us to serve as witnesses, signing our names accordingly. At the request of *(your name)*, and in *(his/her)* presence, and in the presence of each other, all being present at the same time, we have signed our names as witnesses. We declare this to be the will of *(your name)*, and that to the best of our knowledge, *(your name)* is a competent adult and was under no undue influence, duress, or constraint at the time of this signing. Under penalty of perjury, we declare that the foregoing is true and correct.

_____

(witness's signature)

_____

(witness's address)

_____

(witness's signature)

_____

(witness's address)

_____

(witness's signature)

_____

(witness's address)

Sample Will for a Married Person with Minor Children

As you have already learned here, parents of minor children have special issues to consider when they do their estate planning. The following will is a simple example of how some parents might address these issues. Trusts and custodianships are two other possible estate planning tools to help parents provide for minor children. Chapter 5 covers both.

Last Will and Testament
of
(your name)

Clause 1

I, *(your name)*, a resident in *(your city and state of residence)*, being of sound mind and not acting under any duress, fraud, or undue influence of any person, declare this instrument as my Last Will and Testament.

Clause 2: Revocation

I hereby revoke all prior wills and codicils by me.

Clause 3: Identification of Family

My spouse's name is *(name of spouse)*. All references in this will to *(him/her)* or to my spouse shall refer only to *(name of spouse)*.

I have not been married previously.

I am the *(mother/father)* of the following children, all living at the time this will was written and executed:

_____   _____
(name of child)   *(date of birth)*

_____   _____
(name of child)   *(date of birth)*

Clause 4: Appointment of Executor

I appoint *(name of executor)* as executor of this will. If *(he/she)* cannot or will not serve in this capacity, I appoint *(name of substitute executor)* as my substitute executor. In addition to all of the powers allowable under the laws of this state, I authorize and empower my executor to *(itemize all of the additional powers and responsibilities you give your executor)*.

I request that my executor be allowed to act without having to post any bond or other kind of security.

Clause 5: Appointment of Guardian

In the event I shall die leaving any of my children as minors and my spouse does not survive me, I appoint as personal and property guardian of my minor children *(name of guardian)*. If *(he/she)* dies, resigns, or is otherwise unable to serve as personal and property guardian, I appoint *(name of alternate guardian)* as successor guardian.

The guardian shall serve without bond or surety and without the intervention of any court except as required by law.

Clause 6: Disposition of Property

I give all of my property to my spouse, *(spouse's full name)*. If *(he/she)* does not survive me by 30 days, I give that property to my children who survive me, to be divided equally among them by my executor.

Although married people typically leave all of their property to their surviving spouse, you can leave your assets to whomever you want. Therefore, you can designate specific beneficiaries to receive specific assets. Also, you can organize your gift giving into categories such as cash, personal property, and real property, as the previous sample will did.

> Jerry Garcia, lead guitarist and vocalist of The Grateful Dead, made many specific bequests in his will. For example, he provided for his children and his wife and left all of his guitars made by Douglas Erwin to Douglas Erwin.

Clause 7: Residuary Estate

I give the rest of my estate, all the property I own that is not legally disposed of by this will or in some other manner, to *(name of residual beneficiary)*. In the event *(he/she)* does not survive me by 30 days, I give the aforementioned gift to *(name of alternate beneficiary)*. If any primary beneficiary of a shared residuary or specific gift made by me in this will fails to survive me by 30 days, the surviving beneficiaries of that gift shall equally divide between them the deceased beneficiary's share. If all primary beneficiaries of a shared residuary or specific gift fail to survive me by 30 days, that gift shall pass to the alternate beneficiaries named to receive that gift. If the alternate beneficiaries named in this will to receive a specific gift fail to survive me by 30 days, or no such named alternate beneficiaries exist, that gift shall become part of my residuary estate.

Clause 8: Simultaneous Death and Survivorship

If I and *(name of spouse)* die at the same time or under such circumstances that it is difficult or impossible to ascertain which of us died first, my spouse shall be deemed to have predeceased me. No person other than my spouse shall be deemed to have survived me if such person dies within 30 days after me.

Clause 9: Signature

I subscribe my name to this will on the *(date)* day of *(month)*, 20 *(year)*, at *(city, county, and state)*, and declare that I am a legal and competent adult and that I did not enter into or sign this will under duress, constraint, or undue influence.

(your legal signature)

Clause 10: Attestation

On this *(date)* day of *(month)*, 20 *(year)*, *(your name)* declared to us, the undersigned, that this document was *(his/her)* will and asked us to serve as witnesses, signing our names accordingly. At the request of *(your name)*, and in *(his/her)* presence, and in the presence of each other, all being present at the same time, we have signed our names as witnesses. We declare this to be the will of *(your name)*, and that to the best of our knowledge, *(your name)* is a competent adult and was under no undue influence, duress or constraint at the time of this signing. Under penalty of perjury, we declare that the foregoing is true and correct.

_____
(witness's signature)

_____
(witness's address)

_____
(witness's signature)

_____
(witness's address)

_____
(witness's signature)

_____
(witness's address)

Sample Will for a Married Person with No Children

Childless married people may leave relatively more of their estates to their siblings, nieces and nephews, friends, and charities than would married people who probably want to leave most, if not all, of their property to their children.

Last Will and Testament
of
(your name)

Clause 1

I, *(your name)*, a resident in *(your city and state of residence)*, being of sound mind and not acting under any duress, fraud, or undue influence of any person, declare this instrument as my Last Will and Testament.

Clause 2: Revocation

I hereby revoke all prior wills and codicils by me.

Clause 3: Identification of Family

My spouse's name is *(name of spouse)*. All references in this will to *(him/her)* or to my spouse shall refer only to *(name of spouse)*.

I was formerly married to *(name of former spouse)*. That marriage ended by *(specify divorce, annulment, or death)*.

Clause 4: Appointment of Executor

I appoint *(name of executor)* as executor of this will. If *(he/she)* cannot or will not serve in this capacity, I appoint *(name of substitute executor)* as my substitute executor. In addition to all of the powers allowable under the laws of this state, I authorize and empower my executor to *(itemize all the additional powers and responsibilities you give your executor)*.

I request that my executor be allowed to act without having to post any bond or other kind of security.

Clause 5: Disposition of Property

I give all of my property to my spouse, *(spouse's name)*, if *(he/she)* survives me by 30 days. If *(he/she)* does not survive me by 30 days, I distribute all of my property as follows:

I give *(name of beneficiary)* my *(description of property)*, if *(he/she)* survives me by 30 days. If *(he/she)* does not survive me by 30 days, I give the above-described property to *(name of alternate beneficiary)*, if *(he/she)* survives me. If neither of the above persons survives me by 30 days, the above-described property should be disposed of with the residue of my estate.

Repeat the above clause if necessary.

I give the sum of $ *(dollar amount)* to *(name of beneficiary)* if *(he/she)* survives me by 30 days. If *(he/she)* does not survive me by 30 days, I give the same sum of money to *(name of alternate beneficiary)*, if *(he/she)* survives me. If neither of the above persons survives me by 30 days, the above-described property should be disposed of with the residue of my estate.

Repeat the above clause if necessary.

I give my *(description of real estate item)* at *(street address, city, county and state)* to *(name of beneficiary)*, if *(he/she)* survives me by 30 days. If *(he/she)* does not survive me by 30 days, I give the above-described property to *(name of alternate beneficiary)* if *(he/she)* survives me. If neither of the above persons survives me by 30 days, the above-described property should be disposed of with the residue of my estate.

Repeat the above clause as necessary.

Clause 6: Residuary Estate

I give the rest of my estate, all the property I own that is not legally disposed of by this will or in some other manner, to *(name of residual beneficiary)*. In the event *(he/she)* does not survive me by 30 days, I give my residuary estate to *(name of alternate beneficiary)*.

If any primary beneficiary of a shared residuary or specific gift made by me in this will fails to survive me by 30 days, the surviving beneficiaries of that gift shall equally divide between them the deceased beneficiary's share. If all primary beneficiaries of a shared residuary or specific gift fail to survive me by 30 days, that gift shall pass to the alternate beneficiaries named to receive that gift. If the alternate beneficiaries named in this will to receive a specific gift fail to survive me by 30 days, or no such named alternate beneficiaries exist, that gift shall become part of my residuary estate.

Clause 7: Simultaneous Death and Survivorship

If I and *(name of spouse)* die at the same time or under such circumstances that it is difficult or impossible to ascertain which of us died first, my spouse shall be deemed to have predeceased me. No person other than my spouse shall be deemed to have survived me if such person dies within 30 days after me.

This same clause should be in your spouse's will. That way, each will can be probated according to the estate plans you've both set up.

Clause 8: Signature

I subscribe my name to this will on the *(date)* day of *(month)*, 20 *(year)*, at *(city, county, and state)*, and declare that I am a legal and competent adult and that I did not enter into or sign this will under duress, constraint, or undue influence.

(your legal signature)

Clause 9: Attestation

On this *(date)* day of *(month)*, 20 *(year)*, *(your name)* declared to us, the undersigned, that this document was *(his/her)* will and asked us to serve as witnesses, signing our names accordingly. At the request of *(your name)*, and in *(his/her)* presence, and in the presence of each other, all being present at the same time, we have signed our names as witnesses. We declare this to be the will of *(your name)*, and that to the best of our knowledge, *(your name)* is a competent adult and was under no undue influence, duress, or constraint at the time of this signing. Under penalty of perjury, we declare that the foregoing is true and correct.

———————————————
(witness's signature)

———————————————
(witness's address)

———————————————
(witness's signature)

———————————————
(witness's address)

———————————————
(witness's signature)

———————————————
(witness's address)

Sample Will for an Unmarried Person with Minor Children Who Lives with a Partner

This will is very similar to the one for a married person with young children. However, this particular will includes provisions for using the Uniform Gifts or Transfers to Minors Act.

Last Will and Testament
of
(your name)

Clause 1

I, *(your name)*, a resident in *(your city and state of residence)*, being of sound mind and not acting under any duress, fraud, or undue influence of any person, declare this instrument as my Last Will and Testament.

Clause 2: Revocation

I hereby revoke all prior wills and codicils by me.

Clause 3: Identification of Family

I am presently unmarried. I am the *(mother/father)* of the following children, all living at the time this will was written and executed.

_____   _____
(name of child)   *(date of birth)*

_____   _____
(name of child)   *(date of birth)*

I was formerly married to *(name of former spouse)*. This marriage ended by *(specify divorce, annulment, or death)*. The name of my partner is *(name of partner)*, and all references in this will to my partner are to *(him/her)*.

Clause 4: Appointment of Executor

I appoint *(name of executor)* as executor of this will. If *(he/she)* cannot or will not serve in this capacity, I appoint *(name of substitute executor)* as my substitute executor. In addition to all of the powers allowable under the laws of this state, I authorize and empower my executor to *(itemize all of the additional powers and responsibilities you give your executor)*.

I request that my executor be allowed to act without having to post any bond or other kind of security.

Clause 5: Appointment of Guardian

In the event I shall die leaving any of my children as minors, I appoint as personal and property guardian of my minor children *(name of guardian)*. If *(he/she)* dies, resigns or is otherwise unable to serve as personal and property guardian, I appoint *(name of alternate guardian)* as successor guardian.

The guardian shall serve without bond or surety and without the intervention of any court except as required by law.

Clause 6: Disposition of Property

I give *(name of beneficiary)* my *(description of property)* if *(he/she)* survives me by 30 days. If *(he/she)* does not survive me by 30 days, I give the above-described property to *(name of alternate beneficiary)* if *(he/she)* survives me by 30 days. If neither of the above persons survives me, the above-described property should be disposed of with the residue of my estate.

Repeat the above clause as necessary.

I give the sum of $ *(dollar amount)* to *(name of beneficiary)* if *(he/she)* survives me by 30 days. If *(he/she)* does not survive me by 30 days, I give the same sum of money to *(name of alternate beneficiary)* if *(he/she)* survives me by 30 days. If neither of the above persons survives me, this same sum of money should be disposed of with the residue of my estate.

Clause 7: Gifts under the Uniform Gifts or Transfers to Minors Act

All property given in this will to *(name of minor child)* shall be given to *(name of account custodian),* as custodian for *(name of minor child)* under the *(specify Uniform Gifts or Transfers to Minors Act)* of *(your state).* If *(name of custodian)* dies, resigns, or is otherwise unable to serve as custodian, I appoint *(name of successor custodian)* as successor custodian.

You need a clause like this for each custodial account you set up, and each minor child needs his or her own custodial account.

Clause 8: Residuary Estate

I give the rest of my estate, all the property I own that is not legally disposed of by this will or in any other manner, to my partner if *(he/she)* survives me by 30 days. In the event *(he/she)* does not survive me by 30 days, I leave the rest of my estate to my children, to be divided equally among them.

Clause 9: Signature

I subscribe my name to this will on the *(date)* day of *(month),* 20 *(year),* at *(city, county, and state),* and declare that I am a legal and competent adult and that I did not enter into or sign this will under duress, constraint, or undue influence.

_____
(your legal signature)

Clause 10: Attestation

On this *(date)* day of *(month)* 20 *(year), (your name)* declared to us, the undersigned, that this document was *(his/her)* will and asked us to serve as witnesses, signing our names accordingly. At the request of *(your name),* and in *(his/her)* presence, and in the presence of each other, all being present at the same time, we have signed our names as witnesses. We declare this to be the will of *(your name).* and that to the best of our knowledge, *(your name)* is a competent adult and was under no undue influence, duress or constraint at the time of this signing. Under penalty of perjury, we declare that the foregoing is true and correct.

_____

(witness's signature)

_____

(witness's address)

_____

(witness's signature)

_____

(witness's address)

_____

(witness's signature)

_____

(witness's address)

Sample Will for an Unmarried Person with No Children Who Lives with a Partner

Unmarried partners who want to leave money and/or other assets to one another must have a will. Otherwise, if one of them dies without a will, the deceased partner's property would go to his legal heirs according to the laws of his state. The surviving partner would get nothing because state inheritance laws do not recognize unmarried partners.

Last Will and Testament
of
(your name)

Clause 1

I, *(your name)*, a resident in *(your city and state of residence)*, being of sound mind and not acting under any duress, fraud or undue influence of any person, declare this instrument as my Last Will and Testament.

Clause 2: Revocation

I hereby revoke all prior wills and codicils by me.

Clause 3: Identification of Family

I am presently unmarried and have no living children.

The name of my partner is *(name of partner)* and all references in this will to my partner are to *(him/her)*.

Clause 4: Appointment of Executor

I appoint *(name of executor)* as executor of this will. If *(he/she)* cannot or will not serve in this capacity, I appoint *(name of substitute executor)* as my substitute executor. In addition to all of the powers allowable under the laws of this state, I authorize and empower my executor to *(itemize all of the additional powers and responsibilities you give your executor)*.

I request that my executor be allowed to act without having to post any bond or other kind of security.

Clause 5: Disposition of Property

I leave all of my estate to *(name of partner)* if *(he/she)* survives me by 30 days. If *(he/she)* does not survive me by 30 days, my property should be distributed as follows:

I give *(name of beneficiary)* my *(description of property)* if *(he/she)* survives me by 30 days. If *(he/she)* does not survive me by 30 days, I give the above-described property to *(name of alternate beneficiary)* if *(he/she)* survives me. If neither of the above persons survives me, the above-described property should be disposed of with the residue of my estate.

Repeat the above clause if necessary.

I give the sum of $ *(dollar amount)* to *(name of beneficiary)* if *(he/she)* survives me by 30 days. If *(he/she)* does not survive me by 30 days, I give the same sum of money to *(name of alternate beneficiary)* if *(he/she)* survives me. If neither of the above persons survives me by 30 days, the aforementioned sum should be disposed of with the residue of my estate.

Clause 6: Residuary Estate

I give the rest of my estate, all the property I own that is not legally disposed of by this will or in any other manner, to *(name of partner)*. In the event *(he/she)* does not survive me, I give my residuary estate to *(name of charity)*, located at *(address of charity)*.

Clause 7: Signature

I subscribe my name to this will on the *(date)* day of *(month)*, 20 *(year)*, at *(city, county, and state)*, and declare that I am a legal and competent adult and that I did not enter into or sign this will under duress, constraint or undue influence.

(your legal signature)

Clause 8: Attestation

On this *(date)* day of *(month)*, 20 *(year)*, *(your name)* declared to us, the undersigned, that this document was *(his/her)* will and asked us to serve as witnesses, signing our names accordingly. At the request of *(your name)* and in the presence of each other, all being present at the same time, we have signed our names as witnesses. We declare this to be the will of *(your name)*, and that to the best of our knowledge, *(your name)* is a competent adult and was under no undue influence, duress or constraint at the time of this signing. Under penalty of perjury, we declare that the foregoing is true and correct.

_____

(witness's signature)

_____

(witness's address)

_____

(witness's signature)

_____

(witness's address)

_____

(witness's signature)

_____

(witness's address)

Special Clauses

Depending on your estate planning goals and needs, any number of special clauses may be appropriate for your will. Some of the most likely include the ones listed below.

Disinheritance Clause

In your will, you should provide for each of your living children as well as for the children of any of your children who may be deceased—your grandchildren in other words. What you leave each of them can be just a token gift of a few dollars or a small item of personal property. If you don't want to remember one of your children or grandchildren in your will, then you should indicate in your will that you are leaving that particular person nothing in your will. Otherwise, you risk the possibility that one of the people you leave out of your will may contest your will. If there is a contest, a probate court hearing will be held. The judge may decide to give the heir who contested your will a share of your estate or may uphold the provisions in your will.

The following is an example of a clause you can use to disinherit someone:

In this will, I intentionally do not give anything to *(name of person you disinherit)*, who is my *(specify child or grandchild)*.

Exoneration Clause

You can give real property, such as a home or land, to a beneficiary free of all liens, or you can convey it with the debt attached. If you do the latter, your beneficiary becomes responsible for paying off the debt. Therefore, depending on the financial resources of your beneficiary and on your own financial resources, you may want to give the beneficiary a gift of real property free of any associated debt. If so, the following clause might be appropriate:

I give *(description of real property)* free and clear of all debt, including mortgages, trust deeds, liens and any other encumbrances, to *(name of beneficiary)*, if *(he/she)* survives me by 30 days. I direct my executor to pay off, discharge and remove with funds from my residuary estate any and all indebtedness secured by mortgages, trust deeds, liens or other encumbrances existing against the aforementioned property at the time of my death and to obtain the release and discharge of such encumbrances.

Payment of Death and Taxes Clause

It is always best to specify exactly how you want to pay any debts and taxes owed by your estate at the time of your death, especially if you want certain assets to be sold to pay those liabilities. For example, you may want your will to specify that any debts and taxes should be paid by the residue of your estate, as many people do. The following clause expresses that wish:

I direct my executor to pay all my debts and all inheritance, estate or other death taxes out of the residue of my estate.

Proportional Abatement Clause

There may not be enough funds in your estate after you die for your executor to give to all of your beneficiaries exactly what you wanted them to have according to the terms of your will. The shortfall could be due to poor planning on your part; unanticipated claims against your estate; a deteriorated economy that has decreased the value of your assets, and so on. To help avoid this problem, you can include in your will a clause that specifies how you want your estate divided up if its value when you die is less than when you wrote your will. For example, the clause that follows gives each of the beneficiaries in your will a proportionally smaller share of your estate than they would have received had it included enough money and other assets for them to get everything that you had intended for them to have:

Should the net assets of my estate be insufficient to satisfy in full all of the general and specific gifts I have made in this will, I direct that all gifts abate proportionally.

Business-Related Clause

As this book has indicated, if you are a business owner or share a business, your estate planning must address the future of those business interests. Although you may be able to find better estate planning tools than a will to transfer your interest in a business, using your will to do that is an option. Following are three clauses for effecting such a transfer. The first clause is for a sole proprietorship, the second is for a partnership, and the third is for shares of a corporation.

For a Sole Proprietorship:

I give to *(name of beneficiary)*, if *(he/she)* survives me by 30 days, my entire interest in *(name of business)*, a sole proprietorship owned by me, with offices in *(counties and states)*. This gift includes all cash, bank accounts, inventory, equipment, machinery and other property used in connection with the business, upon condition that *(name of beneficiary)* pays or assumes responsibility for any business-related indebtedness I owe at the time of my death.

If *(name of beneficiary)* does not survive me by 30 days or is unwilling to assume all the aforementioned debt, I direct that the aforementioned business be sold and the proceeds disposed of with the residue of my estate.

For a Partnership:

I give to *(name of beneficiary)* if *(he/she)* survives me by 30 days, my entire interest in *(name of business)*, a general partnership of which I am a general partner. This gift includes all my rights to specific partnership property, my rights to a proportionate share of the profits of the partnership, my rights to the return of my capital contributions to the partnership, my rights as a creditor of the partnership and any other rights that I have under a partnership agreement or otherwise as a withdrawing or deceased general partner of the partnership. If *(name of beneficiary)* does not survive me by 30 days, I direct that the aforementioned interest in the aforementioned partnership be liquidated and the proceeds disposed of with the residue of my estate.

For Shares of a Corporation:

I give *(number)* shares of the common stock of *(name of corporation)* to *(name of beneficiary)* if *(he/she)* survives me by 30 days. If *(he/she)* does not survive me by 30 days, I give the aforementioned shares to *(name of alternate beneficiary)*. If neither survives me by 30 days, I direct that the aforementioned shares be disposed of with the residue of my estate. If the capital structure of *(name of corporation)* is changed after the signing of this will, I give to *(name of beneficiary)* the shares acquired by me by reason of ownership of the stock of said corporation through stock splits, stock dividends or the exercise of rights issued to me.

Self-Proving Affidavit

After you die, the court may send a copy of your will to the people who witnessed your signing it along with an affidavit for them to sign and return to the court. In signing the affidavit, they are confirming that the signatures on the will belong to you and to them and that all appropriate legal procedures were followed during the witnessing. Depending on the circumstances after you die, your witnesses may have to come to court to do this.

If the court cannot find the witnesses or if they have died, the probate process will be delayed. To avoid such a delay, most states now allow use of a *self-proving affidavit* that is completed and signed at the same time that you and your witnesses sign your will. A notary public fills out the self-proving affidavit and notarizes it after everyone has signed it. Figure 7.1 shows an example of a self-proving affidavit.

Giving Love and Saying Goodbye

Wills are formal legal documents that reveal very little about the relationships between the person who has written the will and the people remembered in the will. Therefore, we usually have to read between the lines to get such information.

John Lennon of the Beatles was pretty clear about the love he felt for his wife, Yoko Ono. For example, he loved her so much that he changed his name to hers. Also, he refers to her as his "beloved wife" in his will. He left most of his estate to Yoko, named her his executor, and designated Yoko the personal as well as the property guardian for any children they might have together.

FIGURE 7.1
Self-Proving Affidavit

The State of
The County of

We, *(your name)*, *(name of witness)*, and *(name of witness)*, the testator and witnesses, respectively, whose names are signed to the attached or foregoing instrument, being first duty sworn, do hereby declare to the undersigned authority that the testator signed and executed the instrument as his or her last will and that he or she signed willingly or directed another to sign for him or her and he or she executed it as his or her free and voluntary act for the purposes therein expressed; and that each of the witnesses, in the presence and hearing of the testator, signed the will as witnesses and that to the best of his or her knowledge, the testator was at that time 18 or more years of age, of sound mind and under no constraint or undue influence.

———————————————
(your signature)

———————————————
(witness's signature)

———————————————
(witness's signature)

Subscribed, sworn and acknowledged before me by *(your name)*, the testator, subscribed and sworn before me by *(name of witness)* and *(name of witness)*, witnesses, this *(date)* day of *(month)*, 20 *(year)*.

(official seal of notary public)

———————————————
(signature of notary)

Source: Adapted from *All-States Wills and Estate Planning Guide,* 1993 edition. The Judge Advocate General's School, U.S. Army, JA 262, *Legal Assistance Wills Guide,* pages 3-16–3-17 (May 1993). Reprinted by permission of the American Bar Association, Chicago, Illinois.

My philosophy about wills is that when you write yours, there is no reason to limit yourself to just giving away your assets when you can use your will to give so much more to those you care about. You can also use your will to say what is in your heart—something that no standard fill-in-the-blanks clause can express for you. Your heart must be your guide. For those of you who need some suggestions for what words and thoughts you might want to express, here are some ideas:

To a Surviving Spouse

To my wife, *(her name),* I give all the love remaining in my heart. The love I have for you in my soul will travel with me to after-life's next journey. Be assured, my sweet wife, my love for you will extend into eternity. You saw me in failure and success, you saw me at my best and worst, and you saw me unlovable, yet you loved me. I leave you with gratitude that I shared my life with you.

To a Surviving Child

To my son, *(his name),* I give you my full respect and love. I watched you grow and experience more suffering at such an early age than most people experience in a lifetime. I was always so proud of how you bore all the bad times with such mature dignity and strength. I thought of you as a man in a boy's body. I can leave knowing you have everything you need inside you to make a good life for yourself.

To a Surviving Sister

To my sister, *(her name),* I give you all my love. Ever since the first day I saw you as a tiny baby, you have been the perfect little sister. I take with me many wonderful thoughts of our times together when we were growing up and of the special times we've shared as adults. I couldn't ask for more in a sister than what you have been to me.

There is no requirement that you include such a clause in your will. Doing so, however, gives you an opportunity to express your feelings—feelings like respect, love, gratitude, understanding, kindness, and compassion. If you have always felt these sentiments in your heart but have never been able to express them, writing your will gives you the chance.

8

Changing or Revoking Your Will or Trust

To be truly effective, estate planning should be viewed as a dynamic activity. That is, you should review your will periodically to ensure that it continues to reflect the assets you own and your wishes for what will happen to them after you die. Also, you should be sure that it continues to reflect your current family situation. For example, your will should be amended when your family expands with the addition of a new child. If you do not review your will on a regular basis, it may not accomplish what you hoped it would when you die. Therefore, this

> Linda McCartney, mother of four, animal rights crusader, vegetarian, and wife of rock and roll legend Paul McCartney, struggled for two years with breast cancer. At the time of her death in April 1998, Paul McCartney said of Linda, "She was unique and the world is a better place for having known her. Her message of love will live on in our hearts forever." One way Linda McCartney expressed her love for her family was through her will. On July 4, 1996, at the beginning of her illness, she updated her will to ensure that her loved ones would be provided for as she wanted them to be when she died.

chapter explains when to change your will, when to revoke or cancel it, and how to do both.

Reviewing Your Will for Necessary Changes

Keep your will as up-to-date as possible, so it will reflect the changing circumstances in your life as well as the changes in the assets you own. Even if you don't think there have been any important changes in your life, review your will every one to two years. Although you may not have acquired or sold any assets, as you read your will you may realize that you have changed your mind about some of its provisions.

Life events that may require a change to your will include these:

- You have a new child.
- One of the beneficiaries in your will dies.
- Your marital status changes.
- You acquire or dispose of important new assets.
- You take on a substantial amount of new debt or your debt decreases significantly.
- You become a business owner, acquire a share of a business, shut down your business, or sell your business.
- Your executor dies or becomes incapacitated.
- Your minor child's personal or property guardian dies, becomes incapacitated, or is unable to act as guardian for some other reason.
- Your relationship with one of your beneficiaries changes.
- You want to add or subtract a beneficiary.
- You move to a new state, and your will may not be legally valid in your new state of residence.
- A state or federal law that affects estate planning is changed or a new law is adopted.
- You win the lottery!

HOT TIP

When you review your will, you may conclude that you need to use another estate planning tool in addition to having a will.

How to Revise Your Will

You can revise your will any time you want and as many times as you want so long as you are physically and mentally competent when you make the changes. If the change you want to make is relatively minor—that is, you are not changing your entire gift-giving scheme or adding a testamentary trust to your will, for example—you can amend it by preparing a *codicil*. A codicil is simply a written statement of the change you are making. To be considered a legally valid part of your will, the codicil must be dated, witnessed, and notarized according to the laws of your state and it must be kept with your will. Figure 8.1 and Figure 8.2 provide examples of a codicil.

You can write an unlimited number of codicils. However, the more codicils you write, the greater the likelihood that they will create inconsistencies, contradictions, or ambiguities in your will when they are read together. Therefore, it's best to limit the number of codicils to just two per will. If you want to write more than two codicils, revoke your current will and write a new one.

HOT TIP

Handwritten changes to a will may invalidate it. Also, use a pen, not a pencil, to write "revoked" or "canceled" on an out-of-date will. Otherwise, after your death there may be questions about the validity of your new will.

Revoking Your Will

If you prepare a new will, cancel your old will by declaring in the new one that you revoke all previous wills. To be safe, make this statement even if your state law says that you revoke a will simply by destroying it—by ripping it up, burning it, or defacing it, for example.

FIGURE 8.1
Sample Codicil

This sample codicil may not meet the legal requirements of your state. It's provided as an example only.

First Codicil to the
Last Will and Testament
of *(your name)*

I, *(your name)*, of *(city, county, and state)*, hereby make, publish and declare this to be the First Codicil to the Last Will and Testament executed by me on the *(date)* day of *(month)*, 20 *(year)*.

1. Additions to Will
I hereby add the following paragraph to clause *(number of clause)* of my will: *(state exactly what you're adding)*.

Repeat the above if necessary.

2. Revisions to Will
I hereby delete *(state exactly what you're deleting)* from clause *(number of clause)* of my will and replace it with the following: *(state exactly what you're adding)*

Repeat the above if necessary.

3. Revocations to Will
I hereby revoke *(state exactly what you're deleting)* from clause *(number of clause)* of my will.

Repeat the above if necessary.

4. Republication
I hereby remake and republish the unamended portions of my will.
In witness whereof, I hereby sign my name to this codicil on the *(date)* day of *(month)*, 20 *(year)*, at *(city, county, and state)*.

_____
(your signature)

FIGURE 8.2
Sample Codicil

The foregoing instrument, consisting of *(number)* pages, of which this is the last, was on the *(date)* day of *(month)*, 20 *(year)*, signed and published by *(your name)*, the testator, and declared by the testator to be the first codicil to *(his/her)* last will in the presence of each of us, who at the request of *(your name)* and in *(his/her)* presence and in the presence of each other, now subscribe our names as witnesses.

_____
(signature of witness)

_____
(signature of witness)

_____
(name and address of witness)

_____
(name and address of witness)

The State of_____
The County of _____

We, *(your name)*, *(name of witness)*, and *(name of witness)*, the testator and the witnesses, respectively, whose names are signed to the attached or foregoing instrument, being first duly sworn, do hereby declare to the undersigned authority that the testator signed and executed the instrument as the first codicil to his or her last will and that he or she signed willingly and that he or she executed it as his or her free and voluntary act for the purposes therein expressed; and that each of the witnesses, in the presence and hearing of the testator, signed the codicil as witnesses and that to the best of his or her knowledge, the testator was at that time 18 or more years of age, of sound mind and under no constraint or undue influence.

_____
(your signature)

_____
(signature of witness)

_____
(signature of witness)

Subscribed, sworn and acknowledged before me by *(your name)*, the testator, and subscribed and sworn before me by *(name of witness)* and *(name of witness)*, witnesses, this *(date)* day of *(month)*, 20 *(year)*.

(official seal of notary public)

_____
(signature of notary)

HOT TIP

When you review your will for possible changes, it is a good time to also consider whether you want to change the beneficiaries for your insurance policy, retirement benefits plan, 401(k), and for other assets for which you designated a beneficiary.

Changing or Revoking a Trust

The only kind of trust you can change is a revocable trust. If you have set up this kind of trust, you can add or subtract trust assets, add or subtract beneficiaries, change the trustee, add a new provision, amend your instructions for the trustee, and so on.

To modify a trust, you must prepare and date an *amendment* to it, which is a fairly straightforward process. Don't amend a trust simply by altering the original trust agreement. The validity of the change you make may be questioned later. If you want to revoke a trust and write a new one, most states require that you prepare a signed and dated formal cancellation document.

Use an attorney to help you modify or revoke a trust. If you don't, you may make an error that invalidates the change or revocation.

9

Planning for the Possibility of Mental or Physical Incapacitation

If you become fatally ill or injured and can't make your own decisions or let your doctors know what kinds of life-prolonging medical care and treatment you do or don't want, modern medicine and medical technology can keep you alive, sometimes indefinitely, whether the care and treatment you receive reflect your wishes or not. The cost of that care and treatment can deplete your estate. Planning for this possibility should be part of your estate planning.

It is also possible that you may become physically or mentally incapacitated for a limited period and unable to manage your own affairs. Estate planning also includes planning for how decisions related to your business and personal affairs will be made under such circumstances. This type of planning is especially important if you are a business owner and your family depends on the business for its livelihood. Without such planning, your business could be financially damaged or ruined and your family's finances devastated.

This chapter reviews some of the tools you can use to control your health and medical care when you can't speak for yourself. It also discusses tools you can use to ensure that your personal, business, financial, and legal affairs will be well managed if an illness or injury temporarily incapacitates you.

Health Care Planning Is Important

Anyone who has ever been in the hospital or had a relative or close friend hospitalized knows just how quickly the medical bills can add up. Even with good health insurance, a serious illness or accident can eat up your savings and maybe even force you to liquidate valuable assets, thus diminishing the size of your estate. This is especially true if you are critically ill or injured and life-sustaining measures are used to keep you alive as long as possible.

An increasing number of people are dealing with this possibility by preparing health care directives, including a living will and a durable power of attorney for health care. You can use these documents to control the kinds of health care and treatment you will receive if you are terminally ill or critically injured and can't speak for yourself. You may want to prepare health care directives for the following reasons:

- You don't want to be kept alive at all costs.
- You don't want your loved ones to go through the emotional pain of watching you die little by little.
- You don't want to put your loved ones in the position of guessing about the kinds of health care and treatment you would or would not want if you could speak for yourself. You especially don't want them to have to decide whether to end the care and treatment that is keeping you alive.
- You want to spare your loved ones the time and expense involved in petitioning the court to have a conservator appointed to handle your affairs.
- You don't want to see the assets in your estate depleted by costly medical care and treatment.

The federal government encourages the use of health care directives. For example, in 1990 Congress passed the Patient Self-Determination Act, which declares that any facility receiving Medicaid or Medicare monies must provide its patients with written information about health care directives at the time of their admission. It also says that if you prepare a health care directive, the facility caring for you must keep the document with your medical records. Many health care facilities provide their patients with standard forms for preparing their own living will and durable power of attorney for health care.

What Is a Living Will?

A *living will* is a written document that speaks for you if you are too ill or too injured to speak for yourself. It states your wishes regarding the use of various life-sustaining treatments and equipment, including respirators, breathing tubes, cardiac assist pumps, intravenous tubes, artificial nutrition tubes, artificial hydration, dialysis, cardiopulmonary resuscitation, and so on. Your living will can spell out what you *do* want as well as what you *don't* want. You can use it to provide your doctors with "do not resuscitate" instructions, "do all you can" instructions, or something in between.

Preparing a Living Will

You can write your own living will without the help of an attorney by using a living will fill-in-the-blanks form available from a hospital in your area, your local bar association, or your local area agency on aging. Also, several national nonprofit organizations offer living wills specific to each state. One of them is Partnership for Caring. You can download its form at the organization's Web site at <www.partnershipforcaring .org/ad.htm> or by calling 800-989-9455 or 410-962-5454. If you don't order online, Partnership for Caring will charge you a small fee for the living will form. Appendix C includes a sample living will for Texas.

Aging with Dignity is another organization that offers a living will form. Its Five Wishes living will is much more detailed than the one available through Partnership for Caring, but it is not legally valid in every state. At the time this book was written, the Five Wishes living will was legally valid in the following states: Alabama, California, Indiana, Kansas, Kentucky, Nevada, New Hampshire, Ohio, Oklahoma, Oregon, South Carolina, Texas, Utah, Vermont, West Virginia, and Wisconsin. For more information about the Five Wishes living will, or to order a copy of the document, call Aging with Dignity at 850-681-2010 or go to the organization's Web site at <www.agingwithdignity.com>. The cost of the living will is $5 plus handling and shipping charges.

HOT TIP

If you use a fill-in-the-blanks living will, make sure that it is legally valid in your state. Otherwise, it won't be legally enforceable.

Using a standard fill-in-the-blanks form is okay as long as it adheres to the laws of your state. If the form does not allow you to adequately address all of your concerns and preferences, prepare your own living will with the help of an attorney. Figure 9.1 reviews the issues that should be addressed in that living will.

Store your living will in a fireproof safe at home or in a safe-deposit box. Make sure someone besides you knows the combination to the safe or has a key to the safe-deposit box. Also, give a copy of your living will to your spouse, your unmarried partner, a close family mem-

FIGURE 9.1
Preparing a Customized Living Will

If you decide to prepare a customized living will rather than using a fill-in-the-blanks form, be sure to address the following questions:

- Do you want to be hooked up to a respirator or a mechanical ventilator?

- Do you want to be kept alive with the help of artificial feeding or a hydration tube?

- How do you feel about invasive surgery should you become terminally ill or critically injured?

- Do you want treatment such as chemotherapy, radiotherapy, and so on? If you do, is there a point at which you would want treatment to stop?

- Under what conditions would you want or not want life-sustaining measures like cardiopulmonary resuscitation, kidney dialysis, blood transfusions, and so on?

- Do you want to be resuscitated?

> ### H O T   T I P
>
> If you are a resident of more than one state, or if you take an annual vacation in another state besides your state of residence, prepare a living will for both states. You should also execute a legal durable health care power of attorney for both states.

ber, or a good friend. Review the document with whoever has a copy of your living will so you can provide explanations of your wishes as necessary and so that person will feel comfortable if your living will has to be activated.

In most states, you must let your doctor know that you have a living will. Even if that is not a requirement in your state, reviewing your living will with your doctor is an excellent idea. That way you can be sure that your doctor feels comfortable with the wishes you have stated in it. If your doctor does not feel comfortable, you can find a doctor who *will* enforce it. Ask your doctor to keep a copy of your living will with your medical records.

Legal Requirements for Living Wills

Living wills are recognized in all states. However, every state has its own criteria for what makes a living will legally valid and enforceable.

The living will you prepare must also have certain characteristics to be legally valid. Those characteristics are listed in Figure 9.2.

> ### H O T   T I P
>
> It's a good idea to initial and date your living will several times each year to indicate that the will continues to reflect your desires. Doing so helps ensure that your wishes will be honored should the time come to enforce them.

FIGURE 9.2
Characteristics of Most Legally Valid Living Wills

- You must be a legal adult when you write your living will. Depending on your state, the age of legal adulthood is either 18 or 21.

- You must be mentally competent at the time that you write your living will.

- Your living will must be written; no state recognizes an oral living will.

- Two adults must sign, date, and witness your living will. In most states, neither of the adults can be your legal heirs.

- Your living will must be notarized.

Changing or Revoking a Living Will

You can change or revoke your living will whenever you want. However, be sure you do it according to your state's rules for amendments and revocations.

In most states, all you need to do to revoke a living will is write on the document that it's no longer valid. If anyone has a copy of the living will you are invalidating, be sure to get those copies back. Do the same if you registered your living will with your state. Some states require registration.

When Will Your Living Will Be Activated?

Generally, your living will cannot be activated until you are near death and two doctors (sometimes one) have stated in writing that you're unable to make your own decisions and are terminally ill or permanently unconscious. If you are in a great deal of pain but death is not imminent, your living will won't go into effect.

Normally, if your doctor is aware that you have a living will and if the document is legally valid, she is expected to comply with it. However, it is always possible that your doctor may ignore the directives of your living will or delay processing the paperwork required to activate it. Your doctor may do this for several reasons:

- She is uncomfortable with the provisions in your living will.
- Your family does not want your living will to be activated and pressures your doctor not to follow the wishes you expressed in it.
- The two doctors who must state in writing that you are *terminally ill* or *permanently unconscious* and near death before your living will can be activated disagree about the definition of those two terms, or they differ about your medical prognosis.
- The provisions in your living will are too vague to be enforced.

To minimize the chance that your family will interfere with the activation of your living will, you should ask them to read it after it's written, explain your requests, and answer any questions they may have. If your loved ones understand the thinking that went into your living will, they are more apt to respect your wishes.

If you are terminally ill or critically injured and your doctor will not comply with the directives in your living will, your family can ask that you be transferred to a more sympathetic physician. However, switching at this point can be difficult. Therefore, your family may need to consult with an attorney who specializes in elder care law and ultimately the matter might have to be decided in court.

HOT TIP

All states exempt doctors from prosecution if their compliance with a patient's health care directive causes the patient's death. In fact, some states prosecute doctors who won't comply with a patient's wishes.

Enforcing Your Living Will with a Durable Power of Attorney for Health Care

Giving someone a durable power of attorney for heath care is one of the best things you can do to help ensure that your living will is enforced when the time comes. The person who has the power of attorney can speak for you regarding your health care and treatment, and push to have your living will activated if your family or doctor is reluctant to. This person can also make medical and health decisions on your behalf when you are dying. In some states, the person to whom you give a durable power of attorney for health care can also make these same decisions when you are physically or mentally incapacitated but death is not an immediate threat. Therefore, a durable power of attorney for health care is a more comprehensive and powerful legal tool than a living will. Appendix D includes a sample durable power of attorney for health care that is valid in Texas.

H O T   T I P

It's a good idea to prepare a living will and a durable power of attorney for health care at the same time.

The person to whom you give this power must be a legal adult and, obviously, should be someone you trust implicitly and who you feel has the personal strength to make potentially difficult decisions on your behalf. Also, she should be willing to accept the important responsibility you want to entrust her with.

Check with your state attorney general's office or with the medical board in your state or county to find out whether there are any legal restrictions on the person to whom you grant a durable power of attorney for health care. For example, you may be prohibited from giving it to your doctor or your residential care provider.

H O T   T I P

Be sure to tell the person to whom you give a durable power of attorney for health care that if you are put in a nursing home or an assisted-living facility and are later transferred to a hospital, she should make sure that your living will transfers with you. She should also make sure that your doctor is aware of your living will and that it is filed with your medical records.

The best kind of durable power of attorney for health care is one that not only specifies the kinds of medical care and treatment you do and don't want but also spells out your values and personal beliefs in regard to such things as life-sustaining measures, pain, the relative cost of various procedures and treatments, and other quality-of-life issues. You may also want to describe what you consider to be an acceptable quality of life. In your instructions to the person with the power of attorney, be as clear and specific as possible so that nothing is left to interpretation. Furthermore, don't just write down this information; talk about it with the individual to whom you give the power of attorney.

> ## HOT TIP
>
> Think carefully before you give your spouse a durable health care power of attorney. Given your close personal relationship with one another, it may be difficult for him to act dispassionately when the time comes. Also, if your living will dictates an end to life-sustaining treatments and your spouse does not want to comply with your wishes, your doctors will probably be very reluctant to activate your living will.

You can use a fill-in-the-blanks form as long as it meets your state's requirements. You can obtain it from the same organizations that provide a living will form. You can also hire an attorney to prepare a durable power of attorney for health care that reflects your particular needs and concerns. Figure 9.3 outlines the basic steps in preparing a health care directive.

> ## HOT TIP
>
> The more specific your durable power of attorney, the more likely it will be honored.

✓ **FIGURE 9.3**
Basic Steps for Preparing a Health Care Directive

❏ Familiarize yourself with the laws of your state that cover health care directives.

❏ Talk with your doctor to find out whether he or she will honor your wishes. Also, contact the hospital(s) where your doctor practices and ask for the same information.

❏ Review your health care directive with your spouse and/or another close family member or friend. You may also want to review it with your adult children. If you give someone a durable power of attorney for health care, discuss its provisions as well as the provisions of your living will with that person. Answer any questions these people may have, and do what you can to address their concerns.

❏ Sign your health care directive.

❏ Have it witnessed and notarized, if required by your state.

❏ Make copies of your directive and give them to the appropriate people. Let these people know where you are keeping the original.

❏ Store your directive in a safe place.

❏ Make your health care directive readily accessible 365 days a year, 24 hours a day.

❏ Review your directive at least once each year to ensure that you don't want to change anything.

Changing or Revoking a Durable Power of Attorney for Health Care

You can change or revoke a durable power of attorney for health care whenever you wish, as long as you are mentally competent. If you change it, make sure you adhere to the laws of your state. If you revoke it, prepare a formal notice of revocation. Also, if you gave copies of your durable power of attorney for health care to other people, get them back and destroy them.

If You Don't Have a Living Will

If you become critically ill and you don't have a living will, the doctor in charge of your care will decide what treatment you will receive. Most likely, your doctor will do whatever is necessary to sustain your life because that is the focus of your doctor's medical education and professional code of ethics. Furthermore, although your doctor may consult with your spouse and other close family members, the doctor is not obligated to comply with your family's wishes in the absence of a living will.

If your family wants to stop certain kinds of medical care and treatment because it believes you wouldn't want it but your doctor is not willing to comply, a court hearing may be held to resolve the stalemate. That hearing will involve legal costs for your family and may also be emotionally draining for them. Another option for your family is to find a new doctor more sympathetic to its wishes, which may again require involvement of the court. A third option is for your family to petition the court to have a conservator appointed who will make medical decisions for you.

HOT TIP

Depending on your state, one of your family members, usually your spouse, can decide whether life-sustaining measures should be continued.

If you are in a committed but unmarried relationship, and especially if you are in a same-sex relationship, your doctor may not consult with your partner about what to do. The best way to ensure that your partner is consulted is to give him a durable power of attorney for your health care. Your partner should also have a copy of your living will.

Conservators

If your family petitions the court for the appointment of a conservator to make health care decisions for you, a hearing will be held to establish that you are not mentally competent to make these decisions for yourself. If the court agrees with your family, it will appoint a conservator, possibly a family member. This person may have to get the court's approval before being able to make certain decisions, and involving the court slows things down.

Burial or Cremation Instructions and Organ Donation

Writing down your wishes regarding your funeral arrangements can make things easier for your loved ones immediately after your death. Another option is to make your own funeral arrangements and then to write them down. Make sure that your executor and your spouse or unmarried partner know where these instructions are stored.

In your written instructions, indicate whether you want to be buried or cremated and whether you want to donate your organs. Also, describe your funeral or memorial service—who you want to speak, where it should be held, what music you want played, who to invite, and so on. If you have purchased a burial plot and arranged for a casket, record that information too.

H O T   T I P

Neither your family nor your executor is legally bound to follow your burial instructions. Usually, however, you can increase the chance that your wishes will be followed by putting them in writing and then discussing them with your family or partner.

The Uniform Anatomical Gift Act allows you to indicate whether you want your organs to be donated to others after your death. Donating an organ so that someone else may live is perhaps the greatest gift you can give to anyone after you die.

As a part of planning for your death, it is a good idea to obtain an organ donor card from your state's department of motor vehicles. Complete the card and have it witnessed. Keep it in your wallet, Daytimer, checkbook, or whatever you always take with you when you leave your home. In some states, you can become an organ donor when you get or renew your driver's license. Your donation wishes are printed on the back of your license. You can also obtain an organ donor card by contacting the Living Bank (P.O. Box 6725, Houston, TX 77265; 713-528-2971).

Make sure that your doctor, close family members, and the person with the durable power of attorney for your health care are aware of your organ donation plans. Your spouse or some other close family member must sign a form consenting to the donation of your organs after you die. If that family member is unaware of your wishes or disagrees with them, he or she might refuse to sign the form.

HOT TIP

You can state your wishes regarding organ donation in the paperwork you must complete to create a durable power of attorney for health care.

Durable Power of Attorney

It is a good idea to give someone a durable power of attorney in addition to giving someone the power to make health and medical care decisions on your behalf. This person would help manage your financial and business affairs if you are unable to do that because you are too ill or too injured. The person to whom you give the power of attorney for your health care does not need to be the same person as the one to whom you gave a durable power of attorney because each job requires different skills.

HOT TIP

Before you give someone a power of attorney for your personal or business affairs, check with your bank to make sure that the power of attorney document allows immediate access to the funds you have at that bank. If not, prepare whatever other documentation you need to have that access. It is also a good idea to get the bank's written approval of your power of attorney after you've prepared it. That way you can be sure that there will be no snafus if your power of attorney has to be activated.

You can give someone a durable power of attorney that applies to either your general person or your business affairs. It can also be set up to apply to a specific transaction. Regardless of what kind of power of attorney you give someone, you must do it while you are mentally competent and understand your actions.

If your estate is modest and you want to make sure that your personal or business affairs will be well managed if you become incapacitated, a durable power of attorney can be an inexpensive alternative to establishing a trust and naming a trustee to manage your affairs. In fact, a durable power of attorney is sometimes called a *poor man's trust.*

H O T   T I P

The person to whom you give a power of attorney can make *inter vivos* gifts on your behalf if you so direct in the document establishing the power of attorney. Check with an attorney before you do, however, as it is possible that the person with the power of attorney could suffer negative tax consequences.

If you don't give someone a durable power of attorney and you become unable to manage your own affairs, your family can ask the court to appoint a guardian for you. However, like the appointment process for a conservator, the court process can be expensive and emotionally difficult for your family. It can also take time, leaving your affairs in limbo until a guardian is appointed. Also, the person the court appoints as your guardian may not be someone you would want making decisions for you if you could speak on your own behalf.

H O T   T I P

When you establish a durable power of attorney, you must explicitly state that it is durable.

Wills of Famous People

LAST WILL AND TESTAMENT
OF
HUMPHREY BOGART

    I, HUMPHREY BOGART, a resident of the County of Los Angeles, State of California, do hereby make, publish and declare this my Last Will and Testament, and hereby revoke all prior wills and codicils.

    <u>FIRST</u>: I am married to BETTY BOGART (also known as LAUREN BACALL BOGART) and have two children, namely, my son STEPHEN HUMPHREY BOGART, who was born January 6, 1949, and my daughter LESLIE BOGART, who was born August 23, 1952. To the best of my knowledge all property (with the exception of our home) in which I have any interest or which stands in my name is community property of my wife and myself accumulated since the date of our marriage. Our home, although acquired with community funds, is held by my wife and me as joint tenants and therefore is not subject to disposition by this Will. It is my intention by this Will to dispose of all property over which I have any power of disposition or appointment, including specifically my wife's interest in community property as well as my own. If my wife shall elect to take against this Will then I direct that the provisions of Clause SIXTH hereof shall be of no force or effect but that all other provisions of this Will shall be given full effect. I recommend to my wife that

she elect to take under the provisions of this Will as it is my firm conviction that such will be to her best interests.

SECOND: I appoint as executors hereof and as trustees hereunder my wife, BETTY, my friend, A. MORGAN MAREE, JR., and SECURITY-FIRST NATIONAL BANK OF LOS ANGELES, a national banking association. If A. MORGAN MAREE, JR. shall be or become unable or unwilling to act in either or both of said capacities, I direct that he shall be replaced in either or both such capacities, as the case may be, first by JESS S. MORGAN, or if he also shall be or become unable or unwilling to act, then by A. MORGAN MAREE 3RD. If BETTY shall be or become unable or unwilling to act in either or both of said capacities her place shall remain vacant. I direct that none of said four individuals shall be required to provide any bond in either of said capacities, regardless of whether two individuals, or only one, shall be serving at a particular time. I authorize my executors to lease, encumber, exchange or sell the whole or any portion of my estate at public or private sale, with or without notice, subject, however, to such confirmation as may be required by law.

THIRD: I give and bequeath my clothing and personal effects to my wife BETTY if she shall survive me. If she shall not survive me I give and bequeath said property to my friend, A. MORGAN MAREE, JR., with the request that he dispose of the same in such manner as he may believe would comply with my desires.

FOURTH: I give and bequeath to my wife BETTY, if she shall survive me, my jewelry, automobiles and accessories thereto, and such interest as I may have in household furniture, furnishings, equipment and effects of every sort and nature. If BETTY shall fail to survive me said property shall fall into the residue of my estate.

FIFTH: I give and bequeath:
(a) To MAY SMITH the amount of two thousand dollars ($2,000);
(b) To KATHRYN SLOAN the amount of fifteen hundred dollars ($1,500);
provided that said persons, respectively, shall still be in my employ at the time of my decease.

SIXTH: If my wife BETTY shall survive me, I give, devise and bequeath one-half (1/2) of the rest, residue and remainder of my estate to my trustees above named to be held by them in a trust for the following uses and upon the following terms and conditions:
(a) The purpose of this trust shall be to provide for the security and welfare of my beloved wife BETTY during

the remainder of her life. In establishing this trust I am particularly aware of her high earning potential, the impact of income taxes thereon, the standard of living to which she has been accustomed during our marriage, and the uncertainties of the many years during which I hope her life will continue in the event of my decease. With these and other factors in mind, and in order to accomplish the purpose stated at the outset, I direct that my trustees (other than BETTY) shall determine, in their absolute discretion, what portion, if any, of the income of this trust and what portion, if any, of the principal hereof, up to the entire amount of such principal, shall be distributed to BETTY from time to time. Any income not so distributed shall be accumulated and added to principal. In exercising their discretion I require that my trustees (other than BETTY) shall take into consideration the income and other amounts received and to be received by BETTY from sources other than this trust, and having done so shall attempt to provide for her in such manner as will permit her to live in comfort and security for the remainder of her life and in a manner which is as near as may be to the standard to which she has been accustomed during our marriage.

(b) Upon the decease of my wife BETTY the remaining principal and any undistributed income of this trust shall go and be distributed to such persons, in such proportions and upon such terms and conditions as she may designate and appoint by her last will and testament. If she shall fail to make such appointment and designation said principal and undistributed income shall, after payment of the expenses of her funeral and last illness (unless such expenses are provided for from other sources), be added proportionately to the shares then held in trust, and the shares theretofore distributed, pursuant to the provisions of Clause SEVENTH hereof.

(c) If distribution cannot be made pursuant to the immediately preceding paragraph (b) because there shall be no issue of my wife BETTY and me then living, this trust shall continue and the net income thereof shall be paid, in quarterly or other convenient installments, to BETTY's mother, NATALIE GOLDBERG, so long as she shall live, and thereafter in equal shares to BETTY's cousins, JUDITH DAVIS ORSHAN and JOAN DAVIS, so long as they both shall live, and all to their survivor so long as she shall live. Upon the decease of the last survivor of said three persons this trust shall terminate, and the principal and any undistributed income thereof shall go and be distributed to THE HUMPHREY BOGART FOUNDATION.

SEVENTH: From the balance of the rest, residue and remainder of my estate my executors shall pay all federal and state inheritance and estate taxes which shall become payable by reason of or in connection with my decease. No part of such taxes shall be charged against any individual beneficiary or legatee under this Will or against the trust established by Clause SIXTH hereof, or against any recipient of property which passes outside of my probate estate. The balance remaining after payment of said taxes I give, devise and bequeath to my trustees named above to be held by them in trust for the following uses and upon the following terms and conditions:

(a) My trustees shall divide the trust estate into as many separate shares as there shall be at my decease children of mine then living and children of mine then deceased who shall have left issue living at my decease. In making such division the trustees shall not be required to make any physical segregation, and may assign undivided interests to the respective shares. Each of said shares shall constitute a separate trust for all purposes.

(b) My trustees shall distribute to, or expend and apply for the benefit of, the child for whom such trust is held, such part or all of the income of such trust and such part or all of the principal thereof, as the trustees shall from time to time deem proper in their absolute discretion. Any income not so distributed, expended or applied shall be accumulated and added to principal. In exercising such discretion my trustees shall take into account the provisions that my wife BETTY shall be able to make for such child from time to time out of funds available to her and shall be guided as near as may be by the standard of living to which said children have been accustomed during my lifetime. It is my desire that their care, comfort and welfare be adequately provided for during their tender years, that they be afforded every opportunity for such higher education as may be appropriate in view of their interest and ability, and that consideration for their support and maintenance after completion of their education shall be secondary. At the discretion of the trustees distributions of income and/or principal during the minority of a child may be made directly to such child or to my wife BETTY, or to such other person as may have actual custody of such child, for application to the use and benefit of such child. Beginning at the age of twenty-three (23) years and thereafter so long as each child shall live, the entire net income of his trust shall be distributed to him at quarterly or other convenient intervals.

(c) I direct that there shall be paid to each child, on his twenty-third (23rd) birthday or upon his marriage prior to attaining the age of twenty-three (23) years, the amount of twenty-five thousand dollars ($25,000) from the principal of his trust. At any time after a child attains the age of twenty-three (23) years the trustees may in their absolute discretion distribute to such child such portion or portions, up to all, of the principal of the trust being

held for such child as the trustees in their absolute
discretion may deem proper. I direct that in any event the
amounts distributed out of principal of each trust held for
a son of mine shall equal at least one-half (1/2) of the
original principal value of such son's trust by the time
such son attains the age of thirty-five (35) years and that
the entire remaining balance of principal of such son's
trust shall be distributed to him by the time he attains
the age of forty-five (45) years. In the case of each trust
held for a daughter of mine, I direct that in any event the
amounts distributed out of principal shall equal at least
one-half (1/2) of the original principal value of such
daughter's trust by the time she attains the age of forty-
five (45) years.

(d) If any child shall die before receiving full
distribution of his trust, the principal and undistributed
income thereof shall thereupon be held or disposed of as
follows:

(1) If such child shall leave surviving issue the
same shall be held for the benefit of such issue;

(2) In the absence of such issue the same shall be
added to the shares then held in trust for, and those
theretofore distributed to, my other children and issue
of deceased children of mine and in the case of shares
theretofore completely distributed the same shall be
distributed forthwith;

(3) If no child of mine or issue of any deceased
child of mine shall then be living the same shall be
added to the trust created by Clause SIXTH hereof, or if
such trust shall not then exist shall go and be
distributed to my wife BETTY, if she shall then be
living.

(e) If distribution of any trust cannot be made pursuant
to the immediately preceding paragraph (d) because of
failure of any issue and BETTY's failure to survive, said
trust shall continue and the net income thereof shall be
paid, in quarterly or other convenient installments, to my
sister, FRANCES BOGART ROSE, so long as she shall live, and
thereafter to her issue, living from time to time, per
stirpes. This trust shall terminate upon the decease of the
last survivor of my sister FRANCES and all her issue
surviving at the time of my decease, and thereupon the
principal and any undistributed income thereof shall go and
be distributed to THE HUMPHREY BOGART FOUNDATION.

(f) Each share held for the benefit of the issue of a
deceased child of mine, pursuant to paragraph (a) or
subdivision (1) of paragraph (d) of this Clause SEVENTH,
shall be divided into as many parts as there are living
issue of such deceased child, calculated on the principle
of representation. Each part set aside for a beneficiary
over the age of twenty-one (21) years shall be distributed

to such person, free of trust. Each part set aside for a beneficiary under the age of twenty-one (21) years shall continue to be held in trust for such beneficiary until he reaches the age of twenty-one (21) years, whereupon the principal and any undistributed income of such part shall be distributed to such beneficiary; and until such age is attained the income derived from such part shall be distributed to or applied for the benefit of such beneficiary. If such beneficiary shall die before attaining the age twenty-one (21) years the principal and undistributed income of the part held for his benefit shall go and be distributed to such persons and in such proportions as may be provided by his will, or if such provision shall not be made by will the same shall go and be distributed to his heirs. Notwithstanding any of the foregoing provisions none of the trusts established by this Will shall last more than twenty-one (21) years after the decease of the last survivor of my issue who shall be living at the date of my decease, and if upon termination pursuant to this provision any portion of principal or undistributed income of any trust shall not be disposed of by the foregoing provisions of this Will, the same shall go and be distributed free of trust to the person for whom such trust was being held immediately prior to such termination.

EIGHTH: If the circumstances shall ever be such that THE HUMPHREY BOGART FOUNDATION shall become entitled to receive any property pursuant to the provisions of either Clause SIXTH or Clause SEVENTH hereof, or both such Clauses, then I direct my trustees to cause to be formed a non-profit corporation bearing that name to receive such property. Said corporation shall have as its primary purpose the making of grants for the aid of medical research, with special reference to the field of cancer. In other respects the details of organization of said corporation shall be determined by my trustees, but I direct that they shall use their best efforts to cause said corporation to be established in such a manner that it will qualify as a charitable corporation for exemption from federal income tax.

NINTH: The following provisions shall relate to each of the trusts created by Clauses SIXTH and SEVENTH of this Will:
    (a) To carry out the purposes of these trusts and subject to any limitations stated elsewhere in the Will, the trustees are vested with the following powers, in addition to those now or hereafter conferred by law, affecting the trusts:
    My trustees may either maintain, continue or operate, at the risk of the trust estate and not at the risk of the trustees, any business enterprise which may be received from

my estate, or may sell, exchange or otherwise dispose of the whole or any part thereof on such terms and for such property as the trustees may deem best; may retain, hold, maintain or continue any securities, properties or investments which may be received from my estate, whether or not the same be of the character permitted by law for investment of trust funds; in the trustees' sole, absolute and uncontrolled discretion, may grant, bargain, sell, convey, exchange, convert, lease for terms within or extending beyond the duration of these trusts, grant for like terms the right to mine or drill for and remove therefrom gas, oil and/or other minerals;

May borrow money for any trust purpose, upon such terms and conditions as the trustees may deem best; may pledge, encumber by mortgage or deed of trust, assign, partition, divide, subdivide or improve any of the trust estate, all upon such terms and conditions, for such purpose, at such price, and for such consideration as shall be, in the discretion of the trustees, for the best interests of the trust estate and the trust beneficiaries; may invest, reinvest, loan or reloan the trust estate in securities, properties or investments, either of the character permitted by law for the investment of trust funds or otherwise; may execute all instruments that the trustees may deem necessary or proper in the administration of the trusts; upon any division or partial or final distribution of the trust properties, may partition, allot and distribute the trusts assets in undivided interests or in money or in kind, or partly in money and partly in kind; and in any separate trust share or trust fund may hold as an investment an undivided interest in any share of stock or other asset; may make all divisions and distributions required hereunder, without order of any court or the appointment of distributors by any court, including the power to make any valuations, revaluations and allocations necessary in connection therewith, which such valuations and allocations by the trustees shall be final and conclusive as to all beneficiaries hereunder; may determine the distributees upon such evidence as the trustees shall deem proper; may set up reserves out of income for the payment of taxes, assessments, insurance, repairs, fees and other expenses of the trusts;

May determine what is principal or income of the trust estate and which expenses shall be chargeable to income or to principal; may compromise claims by or against the trusts; and generally in all respects may handle, manage and operate the trust estate in such manner and upon such terms and conditions as may, in the absolute and uncontrolled discretion of the trustees, seem best for the trust estate and the beneficiaries interested therein, and may do all of such other things and exercise and execute each and every right, power and privilege in connection with and with relation to the trust estate as could be done, exercised and/or executed by an individual holding and owning such property in absolute and unconditional ownership, including, without limiting the foregoing, the rights as respects stocks and bonds of holding said securities in the trustees' names or otherwise, voting, giving proxies, paying calls for assessments, exchanging securities, selling or exercising stock subscription or conversion rights, participating in foreclosures, reorganizations, consolidations, mergers, liquidations, pooling agreements, voting trusts and assenting to corporate sales or other acts.

(b) The interests of beneficiaries in principal or income shall not be subject to claims of their creditors or others nor to legal process, and may not be voluntarily or involuntarily alienated or encumbered.

(c) Wherever appropriate the masculine shall include the feminine and the singular shall include the plural, and vice versa.

TENTH: I have, except as otherwise specified in the Will, intentionally and with full knowledge omitted to provide for my heirs living at the time of my death. To each of my heirs if any living at the time of my death for whom no provision has been made above, I leave the amount of one dollar ($1.00).

IN WITNESS WHEREOF, I have hereunto set my hand this 6th day of June, 1956 at Los Angeles, California.

[Signature torn from document]

The foregoing instrument, consisting of thirteen (13) pages, including this page, was on the date thereof by the said HUMPHREY BOGART subscribed, published and declared to be his Last Will and Testament, in the presence of us, who, at his request and in his presence, and in the presence of each other, sign the same as witnesses thereto.

_____   Residing at _____

_____

_____   Residing at _____

_____

_____   Residing at _____

_____

LAST WILL AND TESTAMENT
OF
JOHN F. KENNEDY, JR.

I, JOHN F. KENNEDY, JR., of New York, New York, make this my last will, hereby revoking all earlier wills and codicils. I do not by this will exercise any power of appointment.

FIRST: I give all my tangible personal property (as distinguished from money, securities and the like), wherever located, other than my scrimshaw set previously owned by my father, to my wife, Carolyn Bessette-Kennedy, if she is living on the thirtieth day after my death, or if not, by right of representation to my then living issue, or if none, by right of representation to the then living issue of my sister, Caroline Kennedy Schlossberg, or if none, to my said sister, Caroline, if she is then living. If I am survived by issue, I leave said scrimshaw set to my said wife, Carolyn, if she is then living, or if not, by right of representation to my then living issue. If I am not survived by issue, I give said scrimshaw set to my nephew John B.K. Schlossberg, if he is then living, or if not, by right of representation to the then living issue of my said sister, Caroline, or if none, to my said sister, Caroline, if she is then living. I hope that whoever receives my tangible personal property will dispose of certain items of it in accordance with my wishes, however made known, but I impose no trust, condition or enforceable obligation of any kind in this regard.

SECOND: I give and devise all my interest in my cooperative apartment located at 20-26 Moore Street, Apartment 9E, in said New York, including my shares therein and any proprietary leases with respect thereto, to my said wife, Carolyn, if she is living on the thirtieth day after my death.

THIRD: If no issue of mine survive me, I give and devise all my interests in real estate, wherever located, that I own as tenants in common with my said sister, Caroline, or as tenants in common with any of her issue, by right of representation to Caroline's issue who are living on the thirtieth day after my death, or if none, to my said sister, Caroline, if she is then living. References in this Article THIRD to "real estate" include shares in cooperative apartments and proprietary leases with respect thereto.

FOURTH: I give and devise the residue of all the property, of whatever kind and wherever located, that I own at my death to the then trustees of The John F. Kennedy, Jr. 1983 Trust established October 13, 1983 by me, as Donor, of which

John T. Fallon, of Weston, Massachusetts, and I are currently the trustees (the "1983 Trust"), to be added to the principal of the 1983 Trust and administered in accordance with the provisions thereof, as amended by a First Amendment dated April 9, 1987 and by a Second Amendment and Complete Restatement dated earlier this day, and as from time to time hereafter further amended whether before or after my death. I have provided in the 1983 Trust for my children and more remote issue and for the method of paying all federal and state taxes in the nature of estate, inheritance, succession and like taxes occasioned by my death.

FIFTH: I appoint my wife, Carolyn Bessette-Kennedy, as guardian of each child of our marriage during minority. No guardian appointed in this will or a codicil need furnish any surety on any official bond.

SIXTH: I name my cousin Anthony Stanislaus Radziwill as my executor; and if for any reason he fails to qualify or ceases to serve in that capacity, I name my cousin Timothy P. Shriver as my executor in his place. References in this will or a codicil to my "executor" mean the one or more executors (or administrators with this will annexed) for the time being in office. No executor named in this will or a codicil need furnish any surety on any official bond. In any proceeding for the allowance for an account of my executor, I request the Court to dispense with the appointment of a guardian ad litem to represent any person or interest. I direct that in any proceeding relating to my estate, service of process upon any person under a disability shall not be made when another person not under a disability is a party to the proceeding and has the same interest as the person under the disability.

SEVENTH: In addition to other powers, my executor shall have power from time to time at discretion and without license of court: To retain, and to invest and reinvest in, any kind or amount of property; to vote and exercise other rights of security holders; to make such elections for federal and state estate, gift, income and generation-skipping transfer tax purposes as my executor may deem advisable; to compromise or submit to arbitration any matters in dispute; to borrow money, and to sell, mortgage, pledge, exchange, lease and contract with respect to any real or personal property, all without notice to any beneficiary and in such manner, for such consideration and on such terms as to credit or otherwise as my executor may deem advisable, whether or not the effect thereof extends beyond the period of settling my estate; and in distributing my estate, to allot property, whether real or personal, at then current values, in lieu of cash.

WITNESS my hand this 19th day of December, 1997.

_____
John F. Kennedy, Jr.

Signed, sealed, published and declared by the above-named John F. Kennedy, Jr. and for his last will, in the presence of us two who, at his request and in his presence and in the presence of each other, hereto subscribe our names as witnesses, all on the date last above written.

Name   Residence Address

_____   _____

_____   _____

STATE OF NEW YORK)
                  ), ss.
COUNTY OF NEW YORK)

Each of the undersigned, individually and severally being duly sworn, deposes and says:

The within will was subscribed in our presence and sight at the end thereof by John F. Kennedy, Jr., the within named testator, on the 19th day of December, 1997, at 500 Fifth Avenue, New York.

Said testator at the time of making such subscription declared the instrument so subscribed to be his last will.

Each of the undersigned thereupon signed his or her name as a witness at the end of said will at the request of said testator and in his presence and sight and in the presence and sight of each other.

Said testator was, at the time of so executing said will, over the age of 18 years and, in the respective opinions of the undersigned, of sound mind, memory and understanding and not under any restraint or in any respect incompetent to make a will.

The testator, in the respective opinions of the undersigned, could read, write and converse in the English language and was suffering from no defect of sight, hearing or speech, or from any other physical or mental impairment which would affect his capacity to make a valid will. The will was

executed as a single, original instrument and was not executed
in counterparts.

        Each of the undersigned was acquainted with said
testator at such time and makes this affidavit at his request.

        The within will was shown to the undersigned at the time
this affidavit was made, and was examined by each of them as to
the signature of said testator and of the undersigned.

        The foregoing instrument was executed by the testator
and witnessed by each of the undersigned affiants under the
supervision of Robert W. Corcoran, attorney-at-law.

                                        _____

                                        _____

Severally sworn to before me
this 19th day of December, 1997.

_____
Notary Public

LAST WILL AND TESTAMENT
OF
JOHN WINSTON ONO LENNON

    I, JOHN WINSTON ONO LENNON, a resident of the County of New York, State of New York, which I declare to be my domicile do hereby make, publish and declare this to be my Last Will and Testament, hereby revoking all other Wills, Codicils and Testamentary dispositions by me at any time heretofore made.

    FIRST: The expenses of my funeral and the administration of my estate, and all inheritance, estate or succession taxes, including interest and penalties, payable by reason of my death shall be paid out of and charged generally against the principal of my residuary estate without apportionment or proration. My Executor shall not seek contribution or reimbursement for any such payments.

    SECOND: Should my wife survive me, I give, devise and bequeath to her absolutely, an amount equal to that portion of my residuary estate, the numerator and denominator of which shall be determined as follows:

    1. The numerator shall be an amount equal to one-half (1/2) of my adjusted gross estate less the value of all other property included in my gross estate for Federal Estate Tax purposes and which pass or shall have passed to my wife either under any other provision of this Will or in any manner outside of this Will in such manner as to qualify for and be allowed as a marital deduction. The words "pass", "have passed", "marital deduction" and "adjusted gross estate" shall have the same meaning as said words have under those provisions of the United States Internal Revenue Code applicable to my estate.

    2. The denominator shall be an amount representing the value of my residuary estate.

    THIRD: I give, devise and bequeath all the rest, residue and remainder of my estate, wheresoever situate, to the Trustees under a Trust Agreement dated November 12, 1979, which I signed with my wife YOKO ONO, and ELI GARBER as Trustees, to be added to the trust property and held and distributed in accordance with the terms of that agreement and any amendments made pursuant to its terms before my death.

    FOURTH: In the event that my wife and I die under such circumstances that there is not sufficient evidence to determine which of us has predeceased the other, I hereby declare it to be my will that it shall be deemed that I shall have predeceased her and that this, my Will, and any and all of its provisions shall be construed based upon that assumption.

FIFTH: I hereby nominate, constitute and appoint my beloved wife YOKO ONO, to act as the Executor of this my Last Will and Testament. In the event that my beloved wife YOKO ONO shall predecease me or chooses not to act for any reason, I nominate and appoint ELI GARBER, DAVID WARMFLASH and CHARLES PETTIT, in the order named, to act in her place and stead.

SIXTH: I nominate, constitute and appoint my wife YOKO ONO, as the Guardian of the person and property of any children of the marriage who may survive me. In the event that she predeceases me, or for any reason she chooses not to act in that capacity, I nominate, constitute and appoint SAM GREEN to act in her place and stead.

SEVENTH: No person named herein to serve in any fiduciary capacity shall be required to file or post any bond for the faithful performance of his or her duties, in that capacity in this or in any other jurisdiction, any law to the contrary notwithstanding.

EIGHTH: If any legatee or beneficiary under this will or the trust agreement between myself as Grantor and YOKO ONO LENNON and ELI GARBER as Trustees, dated November 12, 1979 shall interpose objections to the probate of the Will, or institute or prosecute or be in any way interested or instrumental in the institution or prosecution of any action or proceeding for the purpose of setting aside or invalidating this Will, then and in each such case, I direct that such legatee or beneficiary shall receive nothing whatsoever under this Will or the aforementioned Trust.

IN WITNESS WHEREOF, I have subscribed and sealed and do publish and declare these presents as and for my Last Will and Testament, this 12th day of November, 1979.

_____ (L.S.)

THE FOREGOING INSTRUMENT consisting of four (4) typewritten pages, including this page, was on the 12th day of November, 1979, signed, sealed, published and declared by JOHN WINSTON ONO LENNON, the Testator therein named, as and for his Last Will and Testament, in the present of us, who at his request, and in his presence, and in the presence of each other, have hereunto set our names as witnesses.

NAME_____   residing at _____

_____

NAME_____   residing at _____

_____

NAME_____   residing at _____

_____

STATE OF NEW YORK   )
) ss.:
COUNTY OF NEW YORK   )

Each of the undersigned, individually and severally being duly sworn, deposes and says:

The within Last Will and Testament was subscribed in our presence and sight at the end thereof by JOHN WINSTON ONO LENNON, the within named Testator, on the 12th day of November, 1979, at One West 72nd Street, New York, New York 10023.

Said Testator at the time of making such subscription declared the instrument so subscribed to be his Last Will and Testament.

Each of the undersigned thereupon signed their names as a witness at the end of said Last Will and Testament at the request of said Testator and in his presence and sight and in the presence and sight of each other.

Said Testator was, at the time of so executing said Last Will and Testament, over the age of 18 years and, in the respective opinions of the undersigned, of sound mind, memory and understanding and not under any restraint or in any respect incompetent to make the Last Will and Testament.

The Testator in the respective opinions of the undersigned, could read, write and converse in the English language and was suffering from no defect of sight, hearing or speech, or from any other physical or mental impairment which would affect his capacity to make a valid Last Will and Testament. The Last Will and Testament was executed as a single, original instrument and was not executed in counterparts.

Each of the undersigned was acquainted with said Testator at such time and makes this affidavit at his request.

The within Last Will and Testament was shown to the undersigned at the time this affidavit was made, and examined by each of them as to the signature of said Testator and of the undersigned.

The foregoing instrument was executed by the Testator and witnessed by each of the undersigned affiants under the supervision of DAVID WARMFLASH, an attorney-at-law.

_____

_____

_____

Severally sworn to before me
this 12th day of November, 1979

_____
Notary Public

LAST WILL AND TESTAMENT
OF
MARILYN MONROE

I, MARILYN MONROE, do make, publish and declare this to be my Last Will and Testament.

FIRST: I hereby revoke all former Wills and Codicils by me made.

SECOND: I direct my Executor, hereinafter named, to pay all of my just debts, funeral expenses and testamentary charges as soon after my death as can conveniently be done.

THIRD: I direct that all succession, estate or inheritance taxes which may be levied against my estate and/or against any legacies and/or devises hereinafter set forth shall be paid out of my residuary estate.

FOURTH: (a) I give and bequeath to BERNICE MIRACLE, should she survive me, the sum of $10,000.00.

(b) I give and bequeath to MAY REIS, should she survive me, the sum of $10,000.00.

(c) I give and bequeath to NORMAN and HEDDA ROSTEN, or to the survivor of them, or if they should both predecease me, then to their daughter, PATRICIA ROSTEN, the sum of $5,000.00, it being my wish that such sum be used for the education of PATRICIA ROSTEN.

(d) I give and bequeath all of my personal effects and clothing to LEE STRASBERG, or if he should predecease me, then to my Executor hereinafter named, it being my desire that he distribute these, in his sole discretion, among my friends, colleagues and those to whom I am devoted.

FIFTH: I give and bequeath to my Trustee, hereinafter named, the sum of $100,000.00, in Trust, for the following uses and purposes:

(a) To hold, manage, invest and reinvest the said property and to receive and collect the income therefrom.

(b) To pay the net income therefrom, together with such amounts of principal as shall be necessary to provide $5,000.00 per annum, in equal quarterly installments, for the maintenance and support of my mother, GLADYS BAKER, during her lifetime.

(c) To pay the net income therefrom, together with such amounts of principal as shall be necessary to provide $2,500.00 per annum, in equal quarterly installments, for the maintenance and support of MRS. MICHAEL CHEKHOV during her lifetime.

(d) Upon the death of the survivor between my mother, GLADYS BAKER, and MRS. MICHAEL CHEKHOV to pay over the principal remaining in the Trust, together with any accumulated income, to DR. MARIANNE KRIS to be used by her for the furtherance of the work of such psychiatric institutions or groups as she shall elect.

SIXTH: All the rest, residue and remainder of my estate, both real and personal, of whatsoever nature and wheresoever situate, of which I shall die seized or possessed or to which I shall be in any way entitled, or over which I shall possess power of appointment by Will at the time of my death, including any lapsed legacies, I give, devise and bequeath as follows:

(a) To MAY REIS the sum of $40,000.00 or 25% of the total remainder of my estate, whichever shall be the lesser.

(b) To DR. MARIANNE KRIS 25% of the balance thereof, to be used by her as set forth in ARTICLE FIFTH (d) of this my Last Will and Testament.

(c) To LEE STRASBERG the entire remaining balance.

SEVENTH: I nominate, constitute and appoint AARON R. FROSCH Executor of this my Last Will and Testament. In the event that he should die or fail to qualify, or resign or for any other reason be unable to act, I nominate, constitute and appoint L. ARNOLD WEISSBERGER in his place and stead.

EIGHTH: I nominate, constitute and appoint AARON R. FROSCH Trustee under this my Last Will and Testament. In the event he should die or fail to qualify, or resign or for any other reason be unable to act, I nominate, constitute and appoint L. ARNOLD WEISSBERGER in his place and stead.

/s/ MARILYN MONROE   (L.S.)
_____

SIGNED, SEALED, PUBLISHED and DECLARED by MARILYN MONROE, the Testatrix above named, as and for her Last Will and Testament, in our presence and we, at her request and in her presence and in the presence of each other, have hereunto subscribed

our names as witnesses this 14th day of January,
One Thousand Nine Hundred Sixty-One.

/s/ AARON R. FROSCH   residing at 10 West 86th St., N.Y.C.

/s/ LOUISE H. WHITE   residing at 209 E.56th St., New York 22, NY

_____   residing at _____

Name	Relationship	Age	Residence
Gladys Eley, aka Gladys Baker	mother	over 21	c/o Inez C. Melson, Conservator of Gladys Eley, aka Gladys Baker, an incompetent 9110 Sunset Boulevard Los Angeles 69, Calif.
Berniece Miracle (named in the Will as Bernice Miracle)	half-sister	over 21	330 S. West 27th St. Gainesville, Florida

WHEREFORE, petitioner prays that the Will of decedent
may be admitted to probate as a foreign will, and that
ancillary letters testamentary be issued to petitioner herein.

Date: Dec. 17, 1962

_____
Aaron R. Frosch

GANG, TYRE, RUDIN & BROWN

By _____

STATE OF NEW YORK   )
) SS.
COUNTY OF NEW YORK)

I, the undersigned, state: That I am the petitioner in
the foregoing proceedings; that I have read the same and know
the contents thereof, and the same is true of my own knowledge,
except as to matters which are therein stated upon information
or belief, and as to those matters that I believe the same to
be true.

Dated: Dec. 17, 1962.

I certify (or declare) under the penalty of perjury that the foregoing is true and correct.

_____

Aaron R. Frosch

<u>LAST WILL AND TESTAMENT OF ELVIS A. PRESLEY, DECEASED</u>
<u>FILED AUGUST 22, 1977</u>
<u>LAST WILL AND TESTAMENT</u>
<u>OF</u>
<u>ELVIS A. PRESLEY</u>

I, ELVIS A. PRESLEY, a resident and citizen of Shelby County, Tennessee, being of sound mind and disposing memory, do hereby make, publish and declare this instrument to be my last will and testament, hereby revoking any and all wills and codicils by me at any time heretofore made.

<u>ITEM I</u>
Debts, Expenses and Taxes

I direct my Executor, hereinafter named, to pay all of my matured debts and my funeral expenses, as well as the costs and expenses of the administration of my estate, as soon after my death as practicable. I further direct that all estate, inheritance, transfer and succession taxes which are payable by reason of my death, whether or not with respect to property passing under this will, be paid out of my residuary estate; and I hereby waive on behalf of my estate any right to recover from any person any part of such taxes so paid. My Executor, in his sole discretion, may pay from my domiciliary estate all or any portion of the costs of ancillary administration and similar proceedings in other jurisdictions.

<u>ITEM II</u>
Instructions Concerning Personal
Property: Enjoyment in Specie

I anticipate that included as a part of my property and estate at the time of my death will be tangible personal property of various kinds, characters and values, including trophies and other items accumulated by me during my professional career. I hereby specifically instruct all concerned that my Executor, herein appointed, shall have complete freedom and discretion as to disposal of any and all such property so long as he shall act in good faith and in the best interest of my estate and my beneficiaries, and his discretion so exercised shall not be subject to question by anyone whomsoever.

I hereby expressly authorize my Executor and my Trustee respectively and successively, to permit any beneficiary of any and all trusts created hereunder to enjoy in specie the use or benefit of any household goods, chattels, or other tangible personal property (exclusive of choses in action, cash, stocks, bonds or other securities) which either my Executor or my

Trustee may receive in kind, and my Executor and my Trustee shall not be liable for any consumption, damage, injury to or loss of any tangible property so used, nor shall the beneficiaries of any trusts hereunder or their executors or administrators be liable for any consumption, damage, injury to or loss of any tangible personal property so used.

<u>ITEM III</u>
Real Estate

If I am the owner of any real estate at the time of my death, I instruct and empower my Executor and my Trustee (as the case may be) to hold such real estate for investment, or to sell same, or any portion thereof, as my Executor or my Trustee (as the case may be) shall in his sole judgment determine to be for the best interest of my estate and the beneficiaries thereof.

<u>ITEM IV</u>
Residuary Trust

After payment of all debts, expenses and taxes as directed under ITEM I hereof, I give, devise and bequeath all the rest, residue, and remainder of my estate, including all lapsed legacies and devises, and any property over which I have a power of appointment, to my Trustee, hereinafter named, in trust for the following purposes:

(a) The Trustee is directed to take, hold, manage, invest and reinvest the corpus of the trust and to collect the income therefrom in accordance with the rights, powers, duties, authority and discretion hereinafter set forth. The Trustee is directed to pay all the expenses, taxes and costs incurred in the management of the trust estate out of the income thereof.

(b) After payment of all expenses, taxes and costs incurred in the management of the trust estate, the Trustee is authorized to accumulate the net income or to pay or apply so much of the net income and such portion of the principal at any time and from time to time for the health, education, support, comfortable maintenance and welfare of: (1) my daughter, Lisa Marie Presley, and any other lawful issue I might have, (2) my grandmother, Minnie Mae Presley, (3) my father, Vernon E. Presley, and (4) such other relatives of mine living at the time of my death who in the absolute discretion of my Trustee are in need of emergency assistance for any of the above mentioned purposes and the Trustee is able to make such distribution without affecting the ability of the trust to meet the present needs of the first three numbered categories of beneficiaries herein mentioned or to meet the reasonably expected future needs of the first three classes of beneficiaries herein mentioned. Any decision of the Trustee as to whether or not distribution shall be made, and also as to the amount of such distribution, to any of the persons described hereunder shall be final and conclusive and not subject to question by any legatee or beneficiary hereunder.

(c) Upon the death of my father, Vernon E. Presley, the Trustee is instructed to make no further distributions to the fourth category of beneficiaries and such beneficiaries shall cease to have any interest whatsoever in this trust.

(d) Upon the death of both my said father and my said grandmother, the Trustee is directed to divide the Residuary Trust into separate and equal trusts, creating one such equal trust for each of my lawful children then surviving and one such equal trust for the living issue collectively, if any, of any deceased child of mine. The share, if any, for the issue of any such deceased child, shall immediately vest in such issue in equal shares but shall be subject to the provisions of ITEM V herein. Separate books and records shall be kept for each trust, but it shall not be necessary that a physical division of the assets be made as to each trust.

The Trustee may from time to time distribute the whole or any part of the net income or principal from each of the aforesaid trusts as the Trustee, in its uncontrolled discretion, considers necessary or desirable to provide for the comfortable support, education, maintenance, benefit and general welfare of each of my children. Such distributions may be made directly to such beneficiary or to any person standing in the place of a parent or to the guardian of the person of such beneficiary and without responsibility on my Trustee to see to the application of any such distributions and in making such distributions, the Trustee shall take into account all other sources of funds known by the Trustee to be available for each respective beneficiary for such purpose.

(e) As each of my respective children attains the age of twenty-five (25) years and provided that both my father and grandmother then be deceased, the trust created hereunder for such child shall terminate, and all the remainder of the assets then contained in said trust shall be distributed to such child so attaining the age of twenty-five (25) years outright and free of further trust.

(f) If any of my children for whose benefit a trust has been created hereunder should die before attaining the age of twenty-five (25) years, then the trust created for such child shall terminate on his death, and all remaining assets then contained in said trust shall be distributed outright and free of further trust and in equal shares to the surviving issue of such deceased child but subject to the provisions of ITEM V herein; but if there be no such surviving issue, then to the brothers and sisters of such deceased child in equal shares, the issue of any other deceased child being entitled collectively to their deceased parent's share. Nevertheless, if any distribution otherwise becomes payable outright and free of trust under the provisions of this paragraph (f) of this ITEM IV of my will to a beneficiary for whom the Trustee is then administering a trust for the benefit of such beneficiary under the provisions of this last will and testament, such distribution shall not be paid outright to such beneficiary but shall be added to and become a part of the trust so being administered for such beneficiary by the Trustee.

ITEM V
Distribution to Minor Children

If any share of corpus of any trust established under this will becomes distributable outright and free of trust to any beneficiary before said beneficiary has attained the age of eighteen (18) years, then said share shall immediately vest in said beneficiary, but the Trustee shall retain possession of such share during the period in which such beneficiary is under the age of eighteen (18) years, and, in the meantime, shall use and expend so much of the income and principal of each share as the Trustee deems necessary and desirable for the care, support and education of such beneficiary, and any income not so expended shall be added to the principal. The Trustee shall have with respect to each share so retained all the power and discretion had with respect to such trust generally.

ITEM VI
Alternate Distributees

In the event that all of my descendants should be deceased at any time prior to the time for the termination of the trusts provided for herein, then in such event all of my estate and all the assets of every trust to be created hereunder (as the case may be) shall then be distributed outright in equal shares to my heirs at law per stirpes.

ITEM VII
Unenforceable Provisions

If any provisions of this will are unenforceable, the remaining provisions shall, nevertheless, be carried into effect.

ITEM VIII
Life Insurance

If my estate is the beneficiary of any life insurance on my life at the time of my death, I direct that the proceeds therefrom will be used by my Executor in payment of the debts, expenses and taxes listed in ITEM I of this will, to the extent deemed advisable by the Executor. All such proceeds not so used are to be used by my Executor for the purpose of satisfying the devises and bequests contained in ITEM IV herein.

ITEM IX
Spendthrift Provision

I direct that the interest of any beneficiary in principal or income of any trust created hereunder shall not be subject to claims of creditors or others, nor to legal process, and may not be voluntarily or involuntarily alienated or encumbered except as herein provided. Any bequests contained herein for any female shall be for her sole and separate use, free from the debts, contracts and control of any husband she may ever have.

ITEM X
Proceeds From Personal Services

All sums paid after my death (either to my estate or to any of the trusts created hereunder) and resulting from personal services rendered by me during my lifetime, including, but not limited to, royalties of all nature, concerts, motion picture contracts, and personal appearances shall be considered to be income, notwithstanding the provisions of estate and trust law to the contrary.

ITEM XI
Executor and Trustee

I appoint as Executor of this, my last will and testament, and as Trustee of every trust required to be created hereunder, my said father.

I hereby direct that my said father shall be entitled by his last will and testament, duly probated, to appoint a successor Executor of my estate, as well as a successor Trustee or successor Trustees of all the trusts to be created under my last will and testament.

If, for any reason, my said father be unable to serve or to continue to serve as Executor and/or as Trustee, or if he be deceased and shall not have appointed a successor Executor or Trustee, by virtue of his last will and testament as stated above, then I appoint National Bank of Commerce, Memphis, Tennessee, or its successor or the institution with which it may merge, as successor Executor and/or as successor Trustee of all trusts required to be established hereunder.

None of the appointees named hereunder, including any appointment made by virtue of the last will and testament of my said father, shall be required to furnish any bond or security for performance of the respective fiduciary duties required hereunder, notwithstanding any rule of law to the contrary.

ITEM XII
Powers, Duties, Privileges and
Immunities of the Trustee

Except as otherwise stated expressly to the contrary herein, I give and grant to the said Trustee (and to the duly appointed successor Trustee when acting as such) the power to do everything he deems advisable with respect to the administration of each trust required to be established under this, my last will and testament, even though such powers would not be authorized or appropriate for the Trustee under statutory or other rules of law. By way of illustration and not in limitation of the generality of the foregoing grant of power and authority of the Trustee, I give and grant to him plenary power as follows:

(a) To exercise all those powers authorized to fiduciaries under the provisions of the Tennessee Code Annotated, Sections 35-616 to 35-618, inclusive, including any amendments thereto in effect at the time of my death, and the same are expressly referred to and incorporated herein by reference.

(b) Plenary power is granted to the Trustee, not only to relieve him from seeking judicial instruction, but to the extent that the Trustee deems it to be prudent, to encourage determinations freely to be made in favor of persons who are the current income beneficiaries. In such instances the rights of all subsequent beneficiaries are subordinate, and the Trustee shall not be answerable to any subsequent beneficiary for anything done or omitted in favor of a current income beneficiary, but no current income beneficiary may compel any such favorable or preferential treatment. Without in anywise minimizing or impairing the scope of this declaration of intent, it includes investment policy, exercise of discretionary power to pay or apply principal and income, and determination of principal and income questions;

(c) It shall be lawful for the Trustee to apply any sum that is payable to or for the benefit of a minor (or any other person who in the judgment of the Trustee, is incapable of making proper disposition thereof) by payments in discharge of the costs and expenses of educating, maintaining and supporting such beneficiary, or to make payment to anyone with whom said beneficiary resides or who has the care or custody of the beneficiary, temporarily or permanently, all without intervention of any guardian or like fiduciary. The receipt of anyone to whom payment is so authorized to be made shall be a complete discharge of the Trustee without obligation on his part to see to the further application thereof, and without regard to other resources that the beneficiary may have, or the duty of any other person to support the beneficiary;

(d) In dealing with the Trustee, no grantee, pledgee, vendee, mortgagee, lessee or other transferee of the trust properties, or any part thereof, shall be bound to inquire with respect to the purpose or necessity of any such disposition or to see to the application of any consideration therefor paid to the Trustee.

ITEM XIII
Concerning the Trustee
And the Executor

(a) If at any time the Trustee shall have reasonable doubt as to his power, authority or duty in the administration of any trust herein created, it shall be lawful for the Trustee to obtain the advice and counsel of reputable legal counsel without resorting to the courts for instructions; and the Trustee shall be fully absolved from all liability and damage or detriment to the various trust estates or any beneficiary thereunder by reason of anything done, suffered or omitted pursuant to advice of said counsel given and obtained in good faith, provided that nothing contained herein shall be construed to prohibit or prevent the Trustee in all proper cases from applying to a court of competent jurisdiction for instructions in the administration of the trust assets in lieu of obtaining advice of counsel.

(b) In managing, investing, and controlling the various trust estates, the Trustee shall exercise the judgment and care under the circumstances then prevailing, which men of prudence, discretion and judgment exercise in the management of their own affairs, not in regard to speculation, but in regard to the permanent disposition of their funds, considering the probable income as well as the probable safety of their capital, and, in addition, the purchasing power of income distribution to beneficiaries.

(c) My Trustee (as well as my Executor) shall be entitled to reasonable and adequate compensation for the fiduciary services rendered by him.

(d) My Executor and his successor Executor shall have the same rights, privileges, powers and immunities herein granted to my Trustee wherever appropriate.

(e) In referring to any fiduciary hereunder, for purposes of construction, masculine pronouns may include a corporate fiduciary or neutral pronouns may include an individual fiduciary.

ITEM XIV
Law Against Perpetuities

(a) Having in mind the rule against perpetuities, I direct that (notwithstanding anything contained to the contrary in this last will and testament) each trust created under this will (except such trusts as have heretofore vested in compliance with such rule or law) shall end, unless sooner terminated under other provisions of this will, twenty-one (21) years after the death of the last survivor of such of the beneficiaries hereunder as are living at the time of my death; and thereupon that the property held in trust shall be distributed free of all trust to the persons then entitled to receive the income and/or principal therefrom, in the proportion in which they are then entitled to receive such income.

(b) Notwithstanding anything else contained in this will to the contrary, I direct that if any distribution under this will becomes payable to a person for whom the Trustee is then administering a trust created hereunder for the benefit of such person, such distribution shall be made to such trust and not to the beneficiary outright, and the funds so passing to such trust shall become a part thereof as corpus and be administered and distributed to the same extent and purpose as if such funds had been a part of such trust at its inception.

ITEM XV
Payment of Estate and
Inheritance Taxes

Notwithstanding the provisions of ITEM X herein, I authorize my Executor to use such sums received by my estate after my death and resulting from my personal services as identified in ITEM X as he deems necessary and advisable in order to pay the taxes referred to in ITEM I of my said will.

        IN WITNESS WHEREOF, I, the said ELVIS A. PRESLEY, do hereunto set my hand and seal in the presence of two (2) competent witnesses, and in their presence do publish and declare this instrument to be my Last Will and Testament, this 3rd day of March, 1977.

_____
ELVIS A. PRESLEY

        The foregoing instrument, consisting of this and eleven (11) preceding typewritten pages, was signed, sealed, published and declared by ELVIS A. PRESLEY, the Testator, to be his Last Will and Testament, in our presence, and we, at his request and in his presence and in the presence of each other, have hereunto subscribed our names as witnesses, this 3rd day of March, 1977, at Memphis, Tennessee.

_____   residing at _____

_____   residing at _____

STATE OF TENNESSEE   )
COUNTY OF SHELBY   )

        _____ and _____, after being first duly sworn, make oath or affirm that the foregoing Last Will and Testament was signed by ELVIS A. PRESLEY and for and at that time acknowledged, published and declared by him to be his Last Will and Testament, in the sight and presence of us, the undersigned, who at his request and in his sight and presence, and in the sight and presence of each other, have subscribed our names as attesting witnesses on the 3rd day of March, 1977, and we further make oath or affirm that the Testator was of sound mind and disposing memory and not acting under fraud, menace or undue influence of any person, and was more than eighteen (18) years of age; and that each of the attesting witnesses is more than eighteen (18) years of age.

_____

_____

        SWORN TO AND SUBSCRIBED before me this 3rd day of March, 1977.

_____
NOTARY PUBLIC

My commission expires:

_____

Admitted to Probate and Ordered Recorded August 22, 1977

JOSEPH W. EVANS, JUDGE

Recorded August 22, 1977
B.J. DUNAVANT, CLERK
BY: Jan Scott, D. C.

B

Important IRS Forms

| Form **706** (Rev. July 1999) Department of the Treasury Internal Revenue Service | **United States Estate (and Generation-Skipping Transfer) Tax Return** Estate of a citizen or resident of the United States (see separate instructions). To be filed for decedents dying after December 31, 1998 For Paperwork Reduction Act Notice, see page 1 of the separate instructions. | OMB No. 1545-0015 |

Part 1.—Decedent and Executor

1a Decedent's first name and middle initial (and maiden name, if any)	1b Decedent's last name	2 Decedent's Social Security No.
3a Legal residence (domicile) at time of death (county, state, and ZIP code, or foreign country)	3b Year domicile established	4 Date of birth	5 Date of death

6a Name of executor (see page 4 of the instructions)

6b Executor's address (number and street including apartment or suite no. or rural route; city, town, or post office; state; and ZIP code)

6c Executor's social security number (see page 4 of the instructions)

7a Name and location of court where will was probated or estate administered | 7b Case number

8 If decedent died testate, check here ▶ ☐ and attach a certified copy of the will. | 9 If Form 4768 is attached, check here ▶ ☐

10 If Schedule R-1 is attached, check here ▶ ☐

Part 2.—Tax Computation

1	Total gross estate less exclusion (from Part 5, Recapitulation, page 3, item 12)	1	
2	Total allowable deductions (from Part 5, Recapitulation, page 3, item 23)	2	
3	Taxable estate (subtract line 2 from line 1)	3	
4	Adjusted taxable gifts (total taxable gifts (within the meaning of section 2503) made by the decedent after December 31, 1976, other than gifts that are includible in decedent's gross estate (section 2001(b)))	4	
5	Add lines 3 and 4	5	
6	Tentative tax on the amount on line 5 from Table A on page 12 of the instructions	6	
7a	If line 5 exceeds $10,000,000, enter the lesser of line 5 or $17,184,000. If line 5 is $10,000,000 or less, skip lines 7a and 7b and enter -0- on line 7c . **7a**		
b	Subtract $10,000,000 from line 7a **7b**		
c	Enter 5% (.05) of line 7b	7c	
8	Total tentative tax (add lines 6 and 7c)	8	
9	Total gift tax payable with respect to gifts made by the decedent after December 31, 1976. Include gift taxes by the decedent's spouse for such spouse's share of split gifts (section 2513) only if the decedent was the donor of these gifts and they are includible in the decedent's gross estate (see instructions)	9	
10	Gross estate tax (subtract line 9 from line 8)	10	
11	Maximum unified credit (applicable credit amount) against estate tax . **11**		
12	Adjustment to unified credit (applicable credit amount). (This adjustment may not exceed $6,000. See page 4 of the instructions.) **12**		
13	Allowable unified credit (applicable credit amount) (subtract line 12 from line 11)	13	
14	Subtract line 13 from line 10 (but do not enter less than zero)	14	
15	Credit for state death taxes. Do not enter more than line 14. Figure the credit by using the amount on line 3 less $60,000. See Table B in the instructions and **attach credit evidence** (see instructions) .	15	
16	Subtract line 15 from line 14	16	
17	Credit for Federal gift taxes on pre-1977 gifts (section 2012) (attach computation) **17**		
18	Credit for foreign death taxes (from Schedule(s) P). (Attach Form(s) 706-CE.) **18**		
19	Credit for tax on prior transfers (from Schedule Q) **19**		
20	Total (add lines 17, 18, and 19)	20	
21	Net estate tax (subtract line 20 from line 16)	21	
22	Generation-skipping transfer taxes (from Schedule R, Part 2, line 10)	22	
23	Total transfer taxes (add lines 21 and 22)	23	
24	Prior payments. Explain in an attached statement **24**		
25	United States Treasury bonds redeemed in payment of estate tax . **25**		
26	Total (add lines 24 and 25)	26	
27	Balance due (or overpayment) (subtract line 26 from line 23)	27	

Under penalties of perjury, I declare that I have examined this return, including accompanying schedules and statements, and to the best of my knowledge and belief, it is true, correct, and complete. Declaration of preparer other than the executor is based on all information of which preparer has any knowledge.

Signature(s) of executor(s) _____ Date _____

_____ Date _____

Signature of preparer other than executor _____ Address (and ZIP code) _____ Date _____

Cat. No. 20548R

Appendix B: Important IRS Forms 191

Form 706 (Rev. 7-99)

Estate of:

Part 3—Elections by the Executor

Please check the "Yes" or "No" box for each question. (See instructions beginning on page 5.)

			Yes	No
1	Do you elect alternate valuation?	**1**		
2	Do you elect special use valuation? If "Yes," you must complete and attach Schedule A–1.	**2**		
3	Do you elect to pay the taxes in installments as described in section 6166? If "Yes," you must attach the additional information described on page 8 of the instructions.	**3**		
4	Do you elect to postpone the part of the taxes attributable to a reversionary or remainder interest as described in section 6163?	**4**		

Part 4—General Information (Note: *Please attach the necessary supplemental documents.* **You must attach the death certificate.)**
(See instructions on page 9.)

Authorization to receive confidential tax information under Regs. sec. 601.504(b)(2)(i); to act as the estate's representative before the IRS; and to make written or oral presentations on behalf of the estate if return prepared by an attorney, accountant, or enrolled agent for the executor:

Name of representative (print or type)	State	Address (number, street, and room or suite no., city, state, and ZIP code)

I declare that I am the ☐ attorney/ ☐ certified public accountant/ ☐ enrolled agent (you must check the applicable box) for the executor and prepared this return for the executor. I am not under suspension or disbarment from practice before the Internal Revenue Service and am qualified to practice in the state shown above.

Signature	CAF number	Date	Telephone number

1 Death certificate number and issuing authority (attach a copy of the death certificate to this return).

2 Decedent's business or occupation. If retired, check here ▶ ☐ and state decedent's former business or occupation.

3 Marital status of the decedent at time of death:

☐ Married

☐ Widow or widower—Name, SSN, and date of death of deceased spouse ▶ --------------------------------

☐ Single
☐ Legally separated
☐ Divorced—Date divorce decree became final ▶

4a Surviving spouse's name	**4b** Social security number	**4c** Amount received (see page 9 of the instructions)

5 Individuals (other than the surviving spouse), trusts, or other estates who receive benefits from the estate (do not include charitable beneficiaries shown in Schedule O) (see instructions). For Privacy Act Notice (applicable to individual beneficiaries only), see the Instructions for Form 1040.

Name of individual, trust, or estate receiving $5,000 or more	Identifying number	Relationship to decedent	Amount (see instructions)

All unascertainable beneficiaries and those who receive less than $5,000 . . . . ▶

Total . . . .

Please check the "Yes" or "No" box for each question.

		Yes	No
6	Does the gross estate contain any section 2044 property (qualified terminable interest property (QTIP) from a prior gift or estate) (see page 9 of the instructions)?		

(continued on next page)

Page 2

Form 706 (Rev. 7-99)

Part 4—General Information (continued)

Please check the "Yes" or "No" box for each question.	Yes	No
7a Have Federal gift tax returns ever been filed?		
If "Yes," please attach copies of the returns, if available, and furnish the following information:		

7b Period(s) covered	7c Internal Revenue office(s) where filed

If you answer "Yes" to any of questions 8–16, you must attach additional information as described in the instructions.

	Yes	No
8a Was there any insurance on the decedent's life that is not included on the return as part of the gross estate?		
b Did the decedent own any insurance on the life of another that is not included in the gross estate?		
9 Did the decedent at the time of death own any property as a joint tenant with right of survivorship in which **(a)** one or more of the other joint tenants was someone other than the decedent's spouse, and **(b)** less than the full value of the property is included on the return as part of the gross estate? If "Yes," you must complete and attach Schedule E		
10 Did the decedent, at the time of death, own any interest in a partnership or unincorporated business or any stock in an inactive or closely held corporation?		
11 Did the decedent make any transfer described in section 2035, 2036, 2037, or 2038 (see the instructions for Schedule G beginning on page 11 of the separate instructions)? If "Yes," you must complete and attach Schedule G		
12 Were there in existence at the time of the decedent's death:		
a Any trusts created by the decedent during his or her lifetime?		
b Any trusts not created by the decedent under which the decedent possessed any power, beneficial interest, or trusteeship?		
13 Did the decedent ever possess, exercise, or release any general power of appointment? If "Yes," you must complete and attach Schedule H		
14 Was the marital deduction computed under the transitional rule of Public Law 97-34, section 403(e)(3) (Economic Recovery Tax Act of 1981)? If "Yes," attach a separate computation of the marital deduction, enter the amount on item 20 of the Recapitulation, and note on item 20 "computation attached."		
15 Was the decedent, immediately before death, receiving an annuity described in the "General" paragraph of the instructions for Schedule I? If "Yes," you must complete and attach Schedule I		
16 Was the decedent ever the beneficiary of a trust for which a deduction was claimed by the estate of a pre-deceased spouse under section 2056(b)(7) and which is not reported on this return? If "Yes," attach an explanation.		

Part 5—Recapitulation

Item number	Gross estate		Alternate value	Value at date of death
1	Schedule A—Real Estate	1		
2	Schedule B—Stocks and Bonds.	2		
3	Schedule C—Mortgages, Notes, and Cash	3		
4	Schedule D—Insurance on the Decedent's Life (attach Form(s) 712) . . .	4		
5	Schedule E—Jointly Owned Property (attach Form(s) 712 for life insurance) .	5		
6	Schedule F—Other Miscellaneous Property (attach Form(s) 712 for life insurance)	6		
7	Schedule G—Transfers During Decedent's Life (att. Form(s) 712 for life insurance)	7		
8	Schedule H—Powers of Appointment	8		
9	Schedule I—Annuities	9		
10	Total gross estate (add items 1 through 9).	10		
11	Schedule U—Qualified Conservation Easement Exclusion	11		
12	Total gross estate less exclusion (subtract item 11 from item 10). Enter here and on line 1 of Part 2—Tax Computation	12		

Item number	Deductions		Amount
13	Schedule J—Funeral Expenses and Expenses Incurred in Administering Property Subject to Claims . . .	13	
14	Schedule K—Debts of the Decedent	14	
15	Schedule K—Mortgages and Liens	15	
16	Total of items 13 through 15	16	
17	Allowable amount of deductions from item 16 (see the instructions for item 17 of the Recapitulation) .	17	
18	Schedule L—Net Losses During Administration	18	
19	Schedule L—Expenses Incurred in Administering Property Not Subject to Claims	19	
20	Schedule M—Bequests, etc., to Surviving Spouse	20	
21	Schedule O—Charitable, Public, and Similar Gifts and Bequests	21	
22	Schedule T—Qualified Family-Owned Business Interest Deduction	22	
23	Total allowable deductions (add items 17 through 22). Enter here and on line 2 of the Tax Computation	23	

Page 3

Form **709**

Department of the Treasury
Internal Revenue Service

United States Gift (and Generation-Skipping Transfer) Tax Return

(Section 6019 of the Internal Revenue Code) (For gifts made during calendar year 2000)

▶ **See separate instructions.**

OMB No. 1545-0020

2000

1 Donor's first name and middle initial	2 Donor's last name	3 Donor's social security number

4 Address (number, street, and apartment number)	5 Legal residence (domicile) (county and state)

6 City, state, and ZIP code	7 Citizenship

Part 1—General Information

		Yes	No
8	If the donor died during the year, check here ▶ ☐ and enter date of death................ , ...		
9	If you received an extension of time to file this Form 709, check here ▶ ☐ and attach the Form 4868, 2688, 2350, or extension letter .		
10	Enter the total number of separate donees listed on Schedule A—count each person only once. ▶		
11a	Have you (the donor) previously filed a Form 709 (or 709-A) for any other year? If the answer is "No," do not complete line 11b .		
11b	If the answer to line 11a is "Yes," has your address changed since you last filed Form 709 (or 709-A)?		
12	Gifts by husband or wife to third parties.—Do you consent to have the gifts (including generation-skipping transfers) made by you and by your spouse to third parties during the calendar year considered as made one-half by each of you? (See instructions.) (If the answer is "Yes," the following information must be furnished and your spouse must sign the consent shown below. **If the answer is "No," skip lines 13–18 and go to Schedule A.**)		

13	Name of consenting spouse	14 SSN		
15	Were you married to one another during the entire calendar year? (see instructions)			
16	If the answer to 15 is "No," check whether ☐ married ☐ divorced or ☐ widowed, and give date (see instructions) ▶			
17	Will a gift tax return for this calendar year be filed by your spouse?			
18	**Consent of Spouse**—I consent to have the gifts (and generation-skipping transfers) made by me and by my spouse to third parties during the calendar year considered as made one-half by each of us. We are both aware of the joint and several liability for tax created by the execution of this consent.			

Consenting spouse's signature ▶   Date ▶

Part 2—Tax Computation

1	Enter the amount from Schedule A, Part 3, line 15	1		
2	Enter the amount from Schedule B, line 3	2		
3	Total taxable gifts (add lines 1 and 2)	3		
4	Tax computed on amount on line 3 (see Table for Computing Tax in separate instructions). . .	4		
5	Tax computed on amount on line 2 (see Table for Computing Tax in separate instructions). . .	5		
6	Balance (subtract line 5 from line 4)	6		
7	Maximum unified credit (nonresident aliens, see instructions)	7	220,550	00
8	Enter the unified credit against tax allowable for all prior periods (from Sch. B, line 1, col. C) . .	8		
9	Balance (subtract line 8 from line 7)	9		
10	Enter 20% (.20) of the amount allowed as a specific exemption for gifts made after September 8, 1976, and before January 1, 1977 (see instructions)	10		
11	Balance (subtract line 10 from line 9)	11		
12	Unified credit (enter the smaller of line 6 or line 11)	12		
13	Credit for foreign gift taxes (see instructions)	13		
14	Total credits (add lines 12 and 13)	14		
15	Balance (subtract line 14 from line 6) (do not enter less than zero)	15		
16	Generation-skipping transfer taxes (from Schedule C, Part 3, col. H, Total)	16		
17	Total tax (add lines 15 and 16).	17		
18	Gift and generation-skipping transfer taxes prepaid with extension of time to file	18		
19	If line 18 is less than line 17, enter **balance due** (see instructions)	19		
20	If line 18 is greater than line 17, enter **amount to be refunded**	20		

Sign Here

Under penalties of perjury, I declare that I have examined this return, including any accompanying schedules and statements, and to the best of my knowledge and belief, it is true, correct, and complete. Declaration of preparer (other than donor) is based on all information of which preparer has any knowledge.

▶ _____   _____
   Signature of donor   Date

Paid Preparer's Use Only

Preparer's signature ▶		Date	Check if self-employed ▶ ☐
Firm's name (or yours if self-employed), address, and ZIP code ▶		Phone no. ▶ ( )	

Attach check or money order here.

For Disclosure, Privacy Act, and Paperwork Reduction Act Notice, see page 11 of the separate instructions for this form.   Cat. No. 16783M   Form **709** (2000)

Form 709 (2000)   Page **2**

SCHEDULE A   **Computation of Taxable Gifts** (Including Transfers in Trust)

A   Does the value of any item listed on Schedule A reflect any valuation discount? If the answer is "Yes," see instructions   . .Yes ☐ No ☐

B   ☐ ◄ Check here if you elect under section 529(c)(2)(B) to treat any transfers made this year to a qualified state tuition program as made ratably over a 5-year period beginning this year. See instructions. Attach explanation.

Part 1—Gifts Subject Only to Gift Tax. *Gifts less political organization, medical, and educational exclusions—see instructions*

A Item number	**B** • Donee's name and address • Relationship to donor (if any) • Description of gift • If the gift was made by means of a trust, enter trust's EIN and attach a description or copy of the trust instrument (see instructions) • If the gift was of securities, give CUSIP number	**C** Donor's adjusted basis of gift	**D** Date of gift	**E** Value at date of gift
1				

Total of Part 1 (add amounts from Part 1, column E) . . . . ▶

Part 2—Gifts That are Direct Skips and are Subject to Both Gift Tax and Generation-Skipping Transfer Tax. You must list the gifts in chronological order. *Gifts less political organization, medical, and educational exclusions—see instructions. (Also list here direct skips that are subject only to the GST tax at this time as the result of the termination of an "estate tax inclusion period." See instructions.)*

A Item number	**B** • Donee's name and address • Relationship to donor (if any) • Description of gift • If the gift was made by means of a trust, enter trust's EIN and attach a description or copy of the trust instrument (see instructions) • If the gift was of securities, give CUSIP number	**C** Donor's adjusted basis of gift	**D** Date of gift	**E** Value at date of gift
1				

Total of Part 2 (add amounts from Part 2, column E) . . . . ▶

Part 3—Taxable Gift Reconciliation

1	Total value of gifts of donor (add totals from column E of Parts 1 and 2)	**1**	
2	One-half of items ....attributable to spouse (see instructions)	**2**	
3	Balance (subtract line 2 from line 1)	**3**	
4	Gifts of spouse to be included (from Schedule A, Part 3, line 2 of spouse's return—see instructions) . .	**4**	
	If any of the gifts included on this line are also subject to the generation-skipping transfer tax, check here ▶ ☐ and enter those gifts also on Schedule C, Part 1.		
5	Total gifts (add lines 3 and 4)	**5**	
6	Total annual exclusions for gifts listed on Schedule A (including line 4, above) (see instructions) . . .	**6**	
7	Total included amount of gifts (subtract line 6 from line 5)	**7**	

Deductions (see instructions)

8	Gifts of interests to spouse for which a marital deduction will be claimed, based on items ----------------------- of Schedule A	**8**		
9	Exclusions attributable to gifts on line 8	**9**		
10	Marital deduction—subtract line 9 from line 8	**10**		
11	Charitable deduction, based on items ----------------less exclusions . .	**11**		
12	Total deductions—add lines 10 and 11		**12**	
13	Subtract line 12 from line 7		**13**	
14	Generation-skipping transfer taxes payable with this Form 709 (from Schedule C, Part 3, col. H, Total) .		**14**	
15	Taxable gifts (add lines 13 and 14). Enter here and on line 1 of the Tax Computation on page 1 . . .		**15**	

(If more space is needed, attach additional sheets of same size.)   Form **709** (2000)

Form 709 (2000) Page **3**

SCHEDULE A Computation of Taxable Gifts *(continued)*

16 Terminable Interest (QTIP) Marital Deduction. (See instructions for line 8 of Schedule A.)

If a trust (or other property) meets the requirements of qualified terminable interest property under section 2523(f), and

   a. The trust (or other property) is listed on Schedule A, and

   b. The value of the trust (or other property) is entered in whole or in part as a deduction on line 8, Part 3 of Schedule A,

then the donor shall be deemed to have made an election to have such trust (or other property) treated as qualified terminable interest property under section 2523(f).

If less than the entire value of the trust (or other property) that the donor has included in Part 1 of Schedule A is entered as a deduction on line 8, the donor shall be considered to have made an election only as to a fraction of the trust (or other property). The numerator of this fraction is equal to the amount of the trust (or other property) deducted on line 10 of Part 3, Schedule A. The denominator is equal to the total value of the trust (or other property) listed in Part 1 of Schedule A.

If you make the QTIP election (see instructions for line 8 of Schedule A), the terminable interest property involved will be included in your spouse's gross estate upon his or her death (section 2044). If your spouse disposes (by gift or otherwise) of all or part of the qualifying life income interest, he or she will be considered to have made a transfer of the entire property that is subject to the gift tax (see Transfer of Certain Life Estates on page 4 of the instructions).

17 Election Out of QTIP Treatment of Annuities

☐ ◄ Check here if you elect under section 2523(f)(6) **NOT** to treat as qualified terminable interest property any joint and survivor annuities that are reported on Schedule A and would otherwise be treated as qualified terminable interest property under section 2523(f). (See instructions.) Enter the item numbers (from Schedule A) for the annuities for which you are making this election ►

SCHEDULE B Gifts From Prior Periods

If you answered "Yes" on line 11a of page 1, Part 1, see the instructions for completing Schedule B. If you answered "No," skip to the Tax Computation on page 1 (or Schedule C, if applicable).

A Calendar year or calendar quarter (see instructions)	B Internal Revenue office where prior return was filed	C Amount of unified credit against gift tax for periods after December 31, 1976	D Amount of specific exemption for prior periods ending before January 1, 1977	E Amount of taxable gifts

1 Totals for prior periods (without adjustment for reduced specific exemption) **1**

2 Amount, if any, by which total specific exemption, line 1, column D, is more than $30,000 . . . . . **2**

3 Total amount of taxable gifts for prior periods (add amount, column E, line 1, and amount, if any, on line 2). (Enter here and on line 2 of the Tax Computation on page 1.) **3**

(If more space is needed, attach additional sheets of same size.)

Form **709** (2000)

Form 709 (2000) Page **4**

SCHEDULE C	Computation of Generation-Skipping Transfer Tax

Note: *Inter vivos direct skips that are completely excluded by the GST exemption must still be fully reported (including value and exemptions claimed) on Schedule C.*

Part 1—Generation-Skipping Transfers

A Item No. (from Schedule A, Part 2, col. A)	B Value (from Schedule A, Part 2, col. E)	C Split Gifts (enter ½ of col. B) (see instructions)	D Subtract col. C from col. B	E Nontaxable portion of transfer	F Net Transfer (subtract col. E from col. D)
1					
2					
3					
4					
5					
6					

If you elected gift splitting and your spouse was required to file a separate Form 709 (see the instructions for "Split Gifts"), you must enter all of the gifts shown on Schedule A, Part 2, of your spouse's Form 709 here. In column C, enter the item number of each gift in the order it appears in column A of your spouse's Schedule A, Part 2. We have preprinted the prefix "S-" to distinguish your spouse's item numbers from your own when you complete column A of Schedule C, Part 3. In column D, for each gift, enter the amount reported in column C, Schedule C, Part 1, of your spouse's Form 709.	Split gifts from spouse's Form 709 (enter item number)	Value included from spouse's Form 709	Nontaxable portion of transfer	Net transfer (subtract col. E from col. D)
	S-			
	S-			
	S-			
	S-			
	S-			
	S-			
	S-			
	S-			

Part 2—GST Exemption Reconciliation (Section 2631) and Section 2652(a)(3) Election

Check box ▶ ☐ if you are making a section 2652(a)(3) (special QTIP) election (see instructions)

Enter the item numbers (from Schedule A) of the gifts for which you are making this election ▶ _____

1	Maximum allowable exemption (see instructions)	1
2	Total exemption used for periods before filing this return	2
3	Exemption available for this return (subtract line 2 from line 1)	3
4	Exemption claimed on this return (from Part 3, col. C total, below)	4
5	Exemption allocated to transfers not shown on Part 3, below. **You must attach a Notice of Allocation.** (See instructions.)	5
6	Add lines 4 and 5	6
7	Exemption available for future transfers (subtract line 6 from line 3)	7

Part 3—Tax Computation

A Item No. (from Schedule C, Part 1)	B Net transfer (from Schedule C, Part 1, col. F)	C GST Exemption Allocated	D Divide col. C by col. B	E Inclusion Ratio (subtract col. D from 1.000)	F Maximum Estate Tax Rate	G Applicable Rate (multiply col. E by col. F)	H Generation-Skipping Transfer Tax (multiply col. B by col. G)
1					55% (.55)		
2					55% (.55)		
3					55% (.55)		
4					55% (.55)		
5					55% (.55)		
6					55% (.55)		
					55% (.55)		
					55% (.55)		
					55% (.55)		

Total exemption claimed. Enter here and on line 4, Part 2, above. May not exceed line 3, Part 2, above		**Total generation-skipping transfer tax.** Enter here, on line 14 of Schedule A, Part 3, and on line 16 of the Tax Computation on page 1	

(If more space is needed, attach additional sheets of same size.)   Form **709** (2000)

Form **709-A**	**United States Short Form Gift Tax Return**	OMB No. 1545-0021

(Rev. November 2000)

Department of the Treasury
Internal Revenue Service

Calendar year 20........

1 Donor's first name and middle initial	**2** Donor's last name	**3** Donor's social security number
4 Address (number, street, and apartment number)		**5** Legal residence (domicile)
6 City, state, and ZIP code		**7** Citizenship

8 Did you file any gift tax returns for prior periods? . . . . ☐ Yes ☐ No

If "Yes," state when and where earlier returns were filed ▶

9 Name of consenting spouse	**10** Consenting spouse's social security number

Note: *Do not use this form to report gifts of closely held stock, partnership interests, fractional interests in real estate, or gifts for which the value has been reduced to reflect a valuation discount. Instead, use Form 709.*

List of Gifts

(a) Donee's name and address and description of gift	(b) Donor's adjusted basis of gift	(c) Date of gift	(d) Value at date of gift

Consent

I consent to have the gifts made by my spouse to third parties during the calendar year considered as made one-half by each of us.

Consenting spouse's signature ▶   **Date** ▶

Sign Here

Under penalties of perjury, I declare that I have examined this return, and to the best of my knowledge and belief, it is true, correct, and complete. Declaration of preparer (other than donor) is based on all information of which preparer has any knowledge.

▶ _____   _____
  Signature of donor   Date

Paid Preparer's Use Only	Preparer's signature ▶	Date	Check if self-employed ▶ ☐
	Firm's name (or yours if self-employed), address, and ZIP code ▶		Phone no. ▶ ( )

For Disclosure, Privacy Act, and Paperwork Reduction Act Notice, see the instructions.   Cat. No. 10171G   Form **709-A** (Rev. 11-2000)

Form **712** (Rev. May 2000) Department of the Treasury Internal Revenue Service	**Life Insurance Statement**	OMB No. 1545-0022

Part I **Decedent—Insured** (To be filed by the executor with **Form 706,** United States Estate (and Generation-Skipping Transfer) Tax Return, or **Form 706-NA,** United States Estate (and Generation-Skipping Transfer) Tax Return, Estate of nonresident not a citizen of the United States.)

1 Decedent's first name and middle initial	2 Decedent's last name	3 Decedent's social security number (if known)	4 Date of death

5 Name and address of insurance company

6 Type of policy	7 Policy number

8 Owner's name. If decedent is not owner, attach copy of application.	9 Date issued	10 Assignor's name. Attach copy of assignment.	11 Date assigned

12 Value of the policy at the time of assignment	13 Amount of premium (see instructions)	14 Name of beneficiaries

15	Face amount of policy	**15** $
16	Indemnity benefits	**16** $
17	Additional insurance	**17** $
18	Other benefits	**18** $
19	Principal of any indebtedness to the company that is deductible in determining net proceeds .	**19** $
20	Interest on indebtedness (line 19) accrued to date of death.	**20** $
21	Amount of accumulated dividends	**21** $
22	Amount of post-mortem dividends	**22** $
23	Amount of returned premium	**23** $
24	Amount of proceeds if payable in one sum	**24** $
25	Value of proceeds as of date of death (if not payable in one sum)	**25** $
26	Policy provisions concerning deferred payments or installments.	

Note: *If other than lump-sum settlement is authorized for a surviving spouse, attach a copy of the insurance policy.*

27	Amount of installments	**27** $
28	Date of birth, sex, and name of any person the duration of whose life may measure the number of payments.	

29	Amount applied by the insurance company as a single premium representing the purchase of installment benefits	**29** $
30	Basis (mortality table and rate of interest) used by insurer in valuing installment benefits.	

----

31 Were there any transfers of the policy within the three years prior to the death of the decedent? . . . ☐ **Yes** ☐ **No**

32 Date of assignment or transfer: ____ / ____ / ____
                                     Month   Day   Year

33 Was the insured the annuitant or beneficiary of any annuity contract issued by the company? . . . . ☐ **Yes** ☐ **No**

34 Did the decedent have any incidents of ownership on any policies on his/her life, but not owned by him/her at the date of death? . . . . ☐ **Yes** ☐ **No**

35 Names of companies with which decedent carried other policies and amount of such policies if this information is disclosed by your records.

The undersigned officer of the above-named insurance company (or appropriate Federal agency or retirement system official) hereby certifies that this statement sets forth true and correct information.

Signature ▶   Title ▶   Date of Certification ▶

Cat. No. 10170V   Form **712** (Rev. 5-2000)

Form 712 (Rev. 5-2000) Page **2**

Part II **Living Insured**

(File with **Form 709,** United States Gift (and Generation-Skipping Transfer) Tax Return. May also be filed with **Form 706,** United States Estate (and Generation-Skipping Transfer) Tax Return, or **Form 706-NA,** United States Estate (and Generation-Skipping Transfer) Tax Return, Estate of nonresident not a citizen of the United States, where decedent owned insurance on life of another.)

SECTION A—General Information

36 First name and middle initial of donor (or decedent)	37 Last name	38 Social security number

39 Date of gift for which valuation data submitted . . . . ▶

40 Date of decedent's death for which valuation data submitted . . . . ▶

SECTION B—Policy Information

41 Name of insured	42 Sex	43 Date of birth

44 Name and address of insurance company

45 Type of policy	46 Policy number	47 Face amount	48 Issue date

49 Gross premium	50 Frequency of payment

51 Assignee's name	52 Date assigned

53 If irrevocable designation of beneficiary made, name of beneficiary	54 Sex	55 Date of birth, if known	56 Date designated

57 If other than simple designation, quote in full. (Attach additional sheets if necessary.)

58 If policy is not paid up:

  a Interpolated terminal reserve on date of death, assignment, or irrevocable designation of beneficiary **58a**

  b Add proportion of gross premium paid beyond date of death, assignment, or irrevocable designation of beneficiary **58b**

  c Add adjustment on account of dividends to credit of policy **58c**

  d Total (add lines 58a, b, and c) **58d**

  e Outstanding indebtedness against policy **58e**

  f Net total value of the policy (for gift or estate tax purposes) (subtract line 58e from line 58d) . . **58f**

59 If policy is either paid up or a single premium:

  a Total cost, on date of death, assignment, or irrevocable designation of beneficiary, of a single-premium policy on life of insured at attained age, for original face amount plus any additional paid-up insurance (additional face amount $ _____) **59a**

    (If a single-premium policy for the total face amount would not have been issued on the life of the insured as of the date specified, nevertheless, assume that such a policy could then have been purchased by the insured and state the cost thereof, using for such purpose the same formula and basis employed, on the date specified, by the company in calculating single premiums.)

  b Adjustment on account of dividends to credit of policy **59b**

  c Total (add lines 59a and 59b) **59c**

  d Outstanding indebtedness against policy **59d**

  e Net total value of policy (for gift or estate tax purposes) (subtract line 59d from line 59c) **59e**

The undersigned officer of the above-named insurance company (or appropriate Federal agency or retirement system official) hereby certifies that this statement sets forth true and correct information.

Signature ▶   Title ▶   Date of Certification ▶

Form **712** (Rev. 5-2000)

Form **8615**

Department of the Treasury
Internal Revenue Service   (99)

**Tax for Children Under Age 14
Who Have Investment Income of More Than $1,400**
▶ Attach only to the child's Form 1040, Form 1040A, or Form 1040NR.
▶ See separate instructions.

OMB No. 1545-0998

2000

Attachment
Sequence No. **33**

Child's name shown on return | Child's social security number

Before you begin: If the child, the parent, or any of the parent's other children under age 14 received capital gains (including capital gain distributions) or farm income, see **Pub. 929,** Tax Rules for Children and Dependents. It explains how to figure the child's tax using the **Capital Gain Tax Worksheet** in the Form 1040 or Form 1040A instructions or **Schedule D** or **J** (Form 1040).

A   Parent's name (first, initial, and last). **Caution:** See instructions before completing.

B Parent's social security number

C   Parent's filing status (check one):
☐ Single   ☐ Married filing jointly   ☐ Married filing separately   ☐ Head of household   ☐ Qualifying widow(er)

Part I   **Child's Net Investment Income**

1	Enter the child's investment income, such as taxable interest, ordinary dividends, and capital gain distributions. See instructions. If this amount is $1,400 or less, **stop;** do not file this form.	**1**	
2	If the child **did not** itemize deductions on **Schedule A** (Form 1040 or Form 1040NR), enter $1,400. If the child **did** itemize deductions, see instructions	**2**	
3	Subtract line 2 from line 1. If the result is zero or less, **stop;** do not complete the rest of this form but **do** attach it to the child's return	**3**	
4	Enter the child's **taxable income** from Form 1040, line 39; Form 1040A, line 25; or Form 1040NR, line 38	**4**	
5	Enter the **smaller** of line 3 or line 4	**5**	

Part II   **Tentative Tax Based on the Tax Rate of the Parent Listed on Line A**

6	Enter the parent's **taxable income** from Form 1040, line 39; Form 1040A, line 25; Form 1040EZ, line 6; TeleFile Tax Record, line K; Form 1040NR, line 38; or Form 1040NR-EZ, line 14. If less than zero, enter -0-	**6**	
	Note: If the total of lines 4 and 6 above is not more than $43,850, lines 7 through 16 may not have to be completed. For details, see the instructions for line 6.		
7	Enter the total net investment income, if any, from Forms 8615, line 5, of **all other** children of the parent identified above. **Do not** include the amount from line 5 above	**7**	
8	Add lines 5, 6, and 7	**8**	
9	Enter the tax on line 8 based on the **parent's** filing status. See instructions. If the **Capital Gain Tax Worksheet** or **Schedule D** or **J** (Form 1040) is used to figure the tax, check here ▶ ☐	**9**	
10	Enter the parent's tax from Form 1040, line 40; Form 1040A, line 26, minus any alternative minimum tax; Form 1040EZ, line 10; TeleFile Tax Record, line K; Form 1040NR, line 39; or Form 1040NR-EZ, line 15. If any tax is from **Form 4972** or **8814,** see instructions. If the **Capital Gain Tax Worksheet** or **Schedule D** or **J** (Form 1040) was used to figure the tax, ... check here ▶ ☐	**10**	
11	Subtract line 10 from line 9 and enter the result. If line 7 is blank, also enter this amount on line 13 and go to **Part III**	**11**	
12a	Add lines 5 and 7	**12a**	
b	Divide line 5 by line 12a. Enter the result as a decimal (rounded to at least three places) . .	**12b**	× .
13	Multiply line 11 by line 12b	**13**	

Part III   **Child's Tax—If lines 4 and 5 above are the same, enter -0- on line 15 and go to line 16.**

14	Subtract line 5 from line 4	**14**	
15	Enter the tax on line 14 based on the **child's** filing status. See instructions. If the **Capital Gain Tax Worksheet** or **Schedule D** or **J** (Form 1040) is used to figure the tax, check here ▶ ☐	**15**	
16	Add lines 13 and 15	**16**	
17	Enter the tax on line 4 based on the **child's** filing status. See instructions. If the **Capital Gain Tax Worksheet** or **Schedule D** or **J** (Form 1040) is used to figure the tax, check here ▶ ☐	**17**	
18	Enter the **larger** of line 16 or line 17 here and on Form 1040, line 40; Form 1040A, line 26; or Form 1040NR, line 39	**18**	

For Paperwork Reduction Act Notice, see page 2 of the instructions.   Cat. No. 64113U   Form **8615** (2000)

Texas Medical Power of Attorney

Reprinted by permission of Partnership for Caring, Inc., 1620 Eye Street, NW, Suite 202, Washington, DC 20006; 800-989-9455.

Texas Medical Power of Attorney

INFORMATION CONCERNING THE MEDICAL POWER OF ATTORNEY

THIS IS AN IMPORTANT LEGAL DOCUMENT. BEFORE SIGNING THIS DOCUMENT, YOU SHOULD KNOW THESE IMPORTANT FACTS:

Except to the extent you state otherwise, this document gives the person you name as your agent the authority to make any and all health care decisions for you in accordance with your wishes, including your religious and moral beliefs, when you are no longer capable of making them yourself. Because "health care" means any treatment, service, or procedure to maintain, diagnose, or treat your physical or mental condition, your agent has the power to make a broad range of health care decisions for you. Your agent may consent, refuse to consent, or withdraw consent to medical treatment and may make decisions about withdrawing or withholding life-sustaining treatment. Your agent may not consent to voluntary inpatient mental health services, convulsive treatment, psychosurgery, or abortion. A physician must comply with your agent's instructions or allow you to be transferred to another physician.

Your agent's authority begins when your doctor certifies that you lack the competence to make health care decisions.

Your agent is obligated to follow your instructions when making decisions on your behalf. Unless you state otherwise, your agent has the same authority to make decisions about your health care as you would have had.

It is important that you discuss this document with your physician or other health care provider before you sign it to make sure that you understand the nature and range of decisions that may be made on your behalf. If you do not have a physician, you should talk with someone else who is knowledgeable about these issues and can answer your questions. You do not need a lawyer's assistance to complete this document, but if there is anything in this document that you do not understand, you should ask a lawyer to explain it to you.

The person you appoint as agent should be someone you know and trust. The person must be 18 years of age or older or a person under 18 years of age who has had the disabilities of minority removed. If you appoint your health or residential care provider (e.g., your physician or an employee of a home health agency, hospital, nursing home, or residential care home, other than a relative), that person has to choose between acting as your agent or as your health or residential care provider; the law does not permit a person to do both at the same time.

You should inform the person you appoint that you want the person to be your health care agent. You should discuss this document with your agent and your physician and give each a signed copy. You should indicate on the document itself the people and institutions who have signed copies. Your agent is not liable for health care decisions made in good faith on your behalf.

Even after you have signed this document, you have the right to make health care decisions for yourself as long as you are able to do so and treatment cannot be given to you or stopped over your objection. You have the right to revoke the authority granted to your agent by informing your agent or your health or residential care provider orally or in writing, or by your execution of a subsequent medical power of attorney. Unless you state otherwise, your appointment of a spouse dissolves on divorce.

This document may not be changed or modified. If you want to make changes in the document, you must make an entirely new one.

You may wish to designate an alternate agent in the event that your agent is unwilling, unable, or ineligible to act as your agent. Any alternate agent you designate has the same authority to make health care decisions for you.

THIS POWER OF ATTORNEY IS NOT VALID UNLESS IT IS SIGNED IN THE PRESENCE OF TWO COMPETENT ADULT WITNESSES. THE FOLLOWING PERSONS MAY NOT ACT AS ONE OF THE WITNESSES:

(1) the person you have designated as your agent;

(2) a person related to you by blood or marriage;

(3) a person entitled to any part of your estate after your death under a will or codicil executed by you or by operation of law;

(4) your attending physician;

(5) an employee of your attending physician;

(6) an employee of your health care facility in which you are a patient if the employee is providing direct patient care to you or is an officer, director, partner, or business office employee of the health care facility or of any parent organization of the health care facility; or

(7) a person who, at the time this power of attorney is executed, has a claim against any part of your estate after your death.

TEXAS MEDICAL POWER OF ATTORNEY

DESIGNATION OF HEALTH CARE AGENT.

I, _____, appoint:

(name)

_____

(name of agent)

_____

(address)

_____

(work telephone number)   *(home telephone number)*

as my agent to make any and all health care decisions for me, except to the extent I state otherwise in this document. This medical power of attorney takes effect if I become unable to make my own health care decisions and this fact is certified in writing by my physician.

LIMITATIONS ON THE DECISION MAKING AUTHORITY OF MY AGENT ARE AS FOLLOWS.

INSTRUCTIONS

PRINT YOUR NAME

PRINT THE NAME, ADDRESS AND HOME AND WORK TELEPHONE NUMBERS OF YOUR AGENT

STATE LIMITATIONS ON YOUR AGENT'S POWER (IF ANY)

© 2000
PARTNERSHIP FOR CARING, INC.

PRINT THE NAME, ADDRESS AND HOME AND WORK TELEPHONE NUMBERS OF YOUR FIRST AND SECOND ALTERNATE AGENTS

FIRST ALTERNATE

SECOND ALTERNATE

LOCATION OF ORIGINAL

© 2000 PARTNERSHIP FOR CARING, INC.

DESIGNATION OF ALTERNATE AGENT.

(You are not required to designate an alternate agent but you may do so. An alternate agent may make the same health care decisions as the designated agent if the designated agent is unable or unwilling to act as your agent. If the agent designated is your spouse, the designation is automatically revoked by law if your marriage is dissolved.)

If the person designated as my agent is unable or unwilling to make health care decisions for me, I designate the following persons to serve as my agent to make health care decisions for me as authorized by this document, who serve in the following order:

A. First Alternate Agent

_____
(name of first alternate agent)

_____
(home address)

_____
(work telephone number)   (home telephone number)

B. Second Alternate Agent

_____
(name of second alternate agent)

_____
(home address)

_____
(work telephone number)   (home telephone number)

The original of this document is kept at: _____

_____

LOCATION OF COPIES

The following individuals or institutions have signed copies:

Name: _____

Address: _____

Name: _____

Address: _____

DURATION.

I understand that this power of attorney exists indefinitely from the date I execute this document unless I establish a shorter time or revoke the power of attorney. If I am unable to make health care decisions for myself when this power of attorney expires, the authority I have granted my agent continues to exist until the time I become able to make health care decisions for myself.

EXPIRATION DATE (IF ANY)

(IF APPLICABLE) This power of attorney ends on the following date:

_____

PRIOR DESIGNATIONS REVOKED.

I revoke any prior medical power of attorney.

ACKNOWLEDGMENT OF DISCLOSURE STATEMENT.

I have been provided with a disclosure statement explaining the effect of this document. I have read and understood that information contained in the disclosure statement.

(YOU MUST DATE AND SIGN THIS POWER OF ATTORNEY)

I sign my name to this medical power of attorney on _____
                                                        (date)

day of _____ _____, at _____.
           (month)   *(year)*   *(city and state)*

PRINT THE DATE

PRINT YOUR LOCATION

SIGN THE DOCUMENT

PRINT YOUR NAME

_____
                    (signature)

_____
                    (print name)

WITNESSING PROCEDURE

YOUR TWO WITNESSES MUST SIGN AND DATE YOUR DOCUMENT BELOW

THEY MUST ALSO PRINT THEIR NAMES AND ADDRESSES

WITNESS #1

WITNESS #2

STATEMENT OF FIRST WITNESS.

I am not the person appointed as agent by this document. I am not related to the principal by blood or marriage. I would not be entitled to any portion of the principal's estate on the principal's death. I am not the attending physician of the principal or an employee of the attending physician. I have no claim against any portion of the principal's estate on the principal's death. Furthermore, if I am an employee of a health care facility in which the principal is a patient, I am not involved in providing direct patient care to the principal and am not an officer, director, partner or business office employee of the health care facility of any parent organization of the health care facility.

Signature: _____

Print Name: _____ Date: _____

Address: _____

SIGNATURE OF SECOND WITNESS

Witness Signature: _____

Print Name: _____ Date: _____

Address: _____

Courtesy of **Partnership for Caring, Inc.**   9/99
1035 30th Street, NW Washington, DC 20007 800-989-9455

D

Texas Directive to Physicians and Family or Surrogates

Reprinted by permission of Partnership for Caring, Inc., 1620 Eye Street, NW, Suite 202, Washington, DC 20006; 800-989-9455.

TEXAS
DIRECTIVE TO PHYSICIANS AND FAMILY
OR SURROGATES

Instructions for completing this document:

This is an important legal document known as an Advance Directive. It is designed to help you communicate your wishes about medical treatment at some time in the future when you are unable to make your wishes known because of illness or injury. These wishes are usually based on personal values. In particular, you may want to consider what burdens or hardships of treatment you would be willing to accept for a particular amount of benefit obtained if you were seriously ill.

You are encouraged to discuss your values and wishes with your family or chosen spokesperson, as well as your physician. Your physician, other health care provider, or medical institution may provide you with various resources to assist you in completing your advance directive. Brief definitions are listed below and may aid you in your discussions and advance planning. Initial the treatment choices that best reflect your personal preferences. Provide a copy of your directive to your physician, usual hospital, and family or spokesperson. Consider a periodic review of this document. By periodic review, you can best assure that the directive reflects your preferences.

In addition to this advance directive, Texas law provides for two other types of directives that can be important during a serious illness. These are the Medical Power of Attorney and the Out-of-Hospital Do-Not-Resuscitate Order. You may wish to discuss these with your physician, family, hospital representative, or other advisers. You may also wish to complete a directive related to the donation of organs and tissues.

DIRECTIVE

PRINT YOUR NAME

I, _____, recognize that the best health care is based upon a partnership of trust and communication with my physician. My physician and I will make health care decisions together as long as I am of sound mind and able to make my wishes known, If there comes a time that I am unable to make medical decisions about myself because of illness or injury, I direct that the following treatment preferences be honored:

TERMINAL CONDITION	**TEXAS DIRECTIVE TO PHYSICIANS AND FAMILY OR SURROGATES — PAGE 2 OF 5**

If, in the judgement of my physician, I am suffering with a terminal condition from which I am expected to die within six months, even with available life-sustaining treatment provided in accordance with prevailing standards of medical care:

TERMINAL CONDITION

INITIAL THE STATEMENT THAT REFLECTS YOUR WISHES

_____ I request that all treatments other than those needed to keep me comfortable be discontinued or withheld and my physician allow me to die as gently as possible; **OR**

_____ I request that I be kept alive in this terminal condition using available life-sustaining treatment. (THIS SELECTION DOES NOT APPLY TO HOSPICE CARE)

IRREVERSIBLE CONDITION

If, in the judgement of my physician, I am suffering with an irreversible condition so that I cannot care for myself or make decisions for myself and am expected to die without life-sustaining treatment provided in accordance with prevailing standards of care:

INITIAL THE STATEMENT THAT REFLECTS YOUR WISHES

_____ I request that all treatments other than those needed to keep me comfortable be discontinued or withheld and my physician allow me to die as gently as possible; **OR**

_____ I request that I be kept alive in this irreversible condition using available life-sustaining treatment. (THIS SELECTION DOES NOT APPLY TO HOSPICE CARE)

STATE SPECIFIC TREATMENT REQUESTS (IF ANY)

Additional requests: (After discussion with your physician, you may wish to consider listing particular treatments in this space that you do or do not want in specific circumstances, such as artificial nutrition and fluids, intravenous antibiotics, etc. Be sure to state whether you do or do not want the particular treatment.)

_____

_____

_____

_____

After signing this directive, if my representative or I elect hospice care, I understand and agree that only those treatments needed to keep me comfortable would be provided and I would not be given available life-sustaining treatments.

DESIGNATION OF A SPOKESPERSON

IF YOU HAVE COMPLETED A MEDICAL POWER OF ATTORNEY DO NOT COMPLETE THIS SECTION

If I do not have a Medical Power of Attorney, and I am unable to make my wishes known, I designate the following person(s) to make treatment decisions with my physician compatible with my personal values:

1. _____
      (name of person)

2. _____
      (name of second person)

(IF A MEDICAL POWER OF ATTORNEY HAS BEEN EXECUTED, THEN AN AGENT HAS BEEN NAMED AND YOU SHOULD NOT LIST ADDITIONAL NAMES IN THIS DOCUMENT.)

If the above persons are not available, or if I have not designated a spokesperson, I understand that the spokesperson will be chosen for me following standards specified in the laws of Texas. If, in the judgement of my physician, my death is imminent within minutes to hours, even with the use of all available medical treatment provided within the prevailing standard of care, I acknowledge that all treatments may be withheld or removed except those needed to maintain my comfort. I understand that under Texas law this directive has no effect if I have been diagnosed as pregnant. This directive will remain in effect until I revoke it. No other person may do so.

SIGN THE DOCUMENT AND PRINT YOUR PLACE OF RESIDENCE

SIGNED _____ **DATE** _____
                      (your name)   (date)

CITY, COUNTY, STATE OF RESIDENCE

_____, _____, _____
        (city)   (county)   (State)

WITNESSES

WITNESSING PROCEDURE

Two competent adult witnesses must sign below, acknowledging the signature of the declarant. The witness designated as Witness 1 may not be a person designated to make a treatment decision for the patient and may not be related to the patient by blood or marriage. This witness may not be entitled to any part of the estate and may not have a claim against the estate of the patient. This witness may not be the attending physician or an employee of the attending physician. If this witness is an employee of a health care facility in which the patient is being cared for, this witness may not be involved in providing direct patient care to the patient. This witness may not be an officer, director, partner, or business office employee of a health care facility in which the patient is being cared for or of any parent organization of the health care facility.   *continued on next page...*

© 2000
PARTNERSHIP FOR CARING, INC.

WITNESS #1

WITNESS #2

WITNESS #1: _____

WITNESS #2: _____

DEFINITIONS OF IMPORTANT TERMS

DEFINITIONS:

"**ARTIFICIAL NUTRITION AND HYDRATION**" means the provision of nutrients or fluids by a tube inserted in a vein, under the skin in the subcutaneous tissues, or in the stomach (gastrointestinal tract).

"**IRREVERSIBLE CONDITION**" means a condition, injury, or illness:
1. that may be treated, but is never cured or eliminated;
2. that leaves a person unable to care for or make decisions for the person's own self; and
3. that, without life-sustaining treatment provided in accordance with the prevailing standard of medical care, is fatal.

EXPLANATION: Many serious illnesses such as cancer, failure of major organs (kidney, heart, liver or lung), and serious brain disease such as Alzheimer's dementia may be considered irreversible early on. There is no cure, but the patient may be kept alive for prolonged periods of time if the patient receives life-sustaining treatments. Late in the course of the same illness, the disease may be considered terminal when, even with treatment, the patient is expected to die. You may wish to consider which burdens of treatment you would be willing to accept in an effort to achieve a particular outcome. This is a very personal decision that you may wish to discuss with your physician, family, or other important persons in your life.

"**LIFE-SUSTAINING TREATMENT**" means treatment that, based on reasonable medical judgement, sustains the life of a patient and without which the patient will die. The term includes both life-sustaining medications and artificial life support such as mechanical breathing machines , kidney dialysis treatment, and artificial hydration and nutrition. The term does not include the administration of pain management medication, the performance of a medical procedure necessary to provide comfort care, or any other medical care provided to alleviate a patient's pain.

DEFINITIONS OF IMPORTANT TERMS (CONTINUED)

"**TERMINAL CONDITION**" means an incurable condition caused by injury, disease, or illness that according to reasonable medical judgement will produce death within six months, even with available life-sustaining treatment provided in accordance with the prevailing standard of medical care.

EXPLANATION: Many serious illnesses may be considered irreversible early in the course of the illness, but they may not be considered terminal until the disease is fairly advanced. In thinking about terminal illness and its treatment, you again may wish to consider the relative benefits and burdens of treatment and discuss your wishes with with your physician, family, or other important persons in your life.

© 2000
PARTNERSHIP FOR CARING, INC.

Glossary

Estate planning has its own vocabulary. Effective estate planning requires that you understand the basics of that vocabulary. This glossary helps you do that.

administrator. The person appointed by a probate court to administer the estate of someone who has died without a will. An administrator plays the same role as an executor.

beneficiary. The person, charitable organization, pet, and so on you choose to leave your money and/or other assets to in your will, in a trust, a custodial account, or the like

bequest. A gift made under or through a will.

bond. A legal document issued by a bonding or insurance company that guarantees that if someone in a position of trust, such as your executor, an account custodian, or a trustee, fails to carry out his legal responsibilities, the company will pay a certain amount of money to whomever is harmed as a result.

bypass trust. A type of trust used in conjunction with the unlimited marital deduction to reduce estate taxes.

codicil. An amendment to your will. Generally, codicils are used to make relatively small changes to your will. A codicil is considered part of your will and to be legally valid must meet your state's legal requirements for a codicil.

community property. Property acquired and income earned by a couple during their marriage and owned jointly by both spouses. In community property states, each spouse has a legal claim to one-half of all of the couple's property. Nine states are community property states—Arizona, California, Idaho, Louisiana, Nevada, New Mexico, Texas, Washington, and Wisconsin. The rest of the states are separate property states.

conservator. Someone appointed by the court to manage the financial affairs of someone else. Also called a guardian.

custodian. The person you name to manage the assets placed in the custodial account you set up for a minor child under the Uniform Gifts to Minors Act or the Uniform Transfers to Minors Act.

death taxes.   Taxes your estate may have to pay after you die depending on its value. They are also referred to as estate taxes.

disinheritance.   Excluding a family member from your will.

equity.   The difference between an asset's current market value and the amount of money that is owed on it.

estate.   Everything that you own at the time of your death.

estate planning.   A multifaceted process that involves planning for the disposal of your assets after you die. It may also include taking steps to minimize the amount of estate taxes your estate must pay and to speed up the transfer of your assets to your beneficiaries. Estate planning also includes writing a living will and giving someone a durable power of attorney for health care.

executor.   The person you name in your will to help settle your estate by taking it through the probate process after your death. Among other things, your executor makes sure that the wishes you express in your will are carried out. Your choice for executor must be officially appointed by the court.

gift tax.   A federal tax applied to *inter vivos* gifts. You get an annual gift tax exclusion of $10,000 ($20,000 if you and your spouse make a gift as a couple). The exclusion applies to as many individuals and organizations as you want to give to in any year. Gifts that are protected by the annual gift tax exclusion are not taxable and do not use up any of your unified gift and estate tax credit.

heir.   A relative who is legally entitled, according to your state's laws, to inherit from your estate if you die without a will.

holographic will.   A handwritten will.

inheritance tax.   A tax paid by the beneficiary of an estate in some states.

***inter vivos* gift.**   A gift that you make to a beneficiary while you are alive.

***inter vivos* trust.**   Another name for a living trust.

intestate.   Dying without a legally valid will.

irrevocable trust.   A trust that cannot be changed once it is set up.

joint tenancy.   A form of property ownership that allows two or more people to own an asset together. One owner cannot give away his share of the property without the other owner's consent; and if one of the owners dies, the other owner(s) automatically own(s) the deceased's share. Married people often own property this way, as do unmarried partners.

living trust.   A trust that you set up while you are alive. It can be irrevocable or revocable, although most living trusts are revocable.

living will.   A kind of health care directive that spells out your wishes regarding the specific types of end-of-life care and treatment you do and do not want.

marital exemption.   A federal tax exemption that allows one spouse to pass all of his estate to the other spouse without any estate tax implications.

minor child.   A child who is younger than 18 or 21 depending on the state.

payable-on-death account.   A bank account trust you can use to leave funds to the account beneficiary. Also known as a Totten trust.

personal guardian.   The person you name in your will to raise your minor child should you and the child's other parent both die.

personal property.   Everything you own other than real property, which includes your home, other buildings, and land.

power of attorney.   A legal document that gives someone the right to act on your behalf. The power of attorney may give someone else the right to make financial decisions or health and medical care decisions for you. A power of attorney can give someone else a onetime, temporary right to make decisions for you or it can be a durable power that means it lasts until you take it away.

probate. The legal process that proves the validity of your will, officially appoints your executor, pays your estates taxes if any are due, pays any legitimate creditor claims against your estate, and distributes the property in your will to your beneficiaries according to the terms of your will.

probate estate. All of the assets that you own that will go through the probate process.

property guardian. The person you name in your will to manage the property you leave your minor child should you die before your child is a legal adult.

real property. Real estate that includes homes and other buildings as well as land.

residuary beneficiary. The beneficiary named in your will who is entitled to receive any of the assets in your probate estate that are not specifically left to another beneficiary in your will after all legitimate claims against your estate have been paid.

residuary estate. The assets left in your estate after all the assets with specific beneficiaries have been distributed. Also called the residue of the estate. These assets go to whomever you designate as the residuary beneficiary.

revocable trust. A living trust that can be modified or even canceled after it is set up.

self-proving will. A will that includes a sworn statement from witnesses that it has been notarized.

settlor. The formal term for someone who creates a trust. Other terms used to describe this same person include trustor, grantor, and donor.

taking against the will. An option given to surviving spouses to inherit a state-determined amount of their deceased spouse's estate rather than whatever the deceased left them in their will.

taxable estate. The assets in your estate that are subject to federal and state estate taxes after your death.

tenancy by the entirety. A form of joint ownership that is available in some states to spouses only.

tenants in common. A type of joint property ownership that gives each owner a share of an asset without an interest in the shares of the other owner(s) or the right of survivorship. Each owner can sell or give away her share without the consent of the other owners.

testamentary trust. A trust that is part of your will and that is not funded until your death.

testator. The person who writes a will.

trust. A legal entity that you can create to own and manage assets for the benefit of one or more beneficiaries. The trust property is managed by a trustee and the trust beneficiaries take control of the property at a time specified in the document that establishes the trust.

trustee. The person who is named in the trust document to manage the trust assets.

Uniform Gifts to Minors Act or Uniform Transfers to Minors Act. Federal laws that permit you to establish a custodial account for a minor child and to place certain types of assets in the account. A custodian manages those assets until the minor reaches 18 or 21.

will. A legal document that spells out what you want to have happen to the assets you own after you die. If you are the parent of a minor child, you can use your will to designate both a personal and a property guardian for the child.

Index